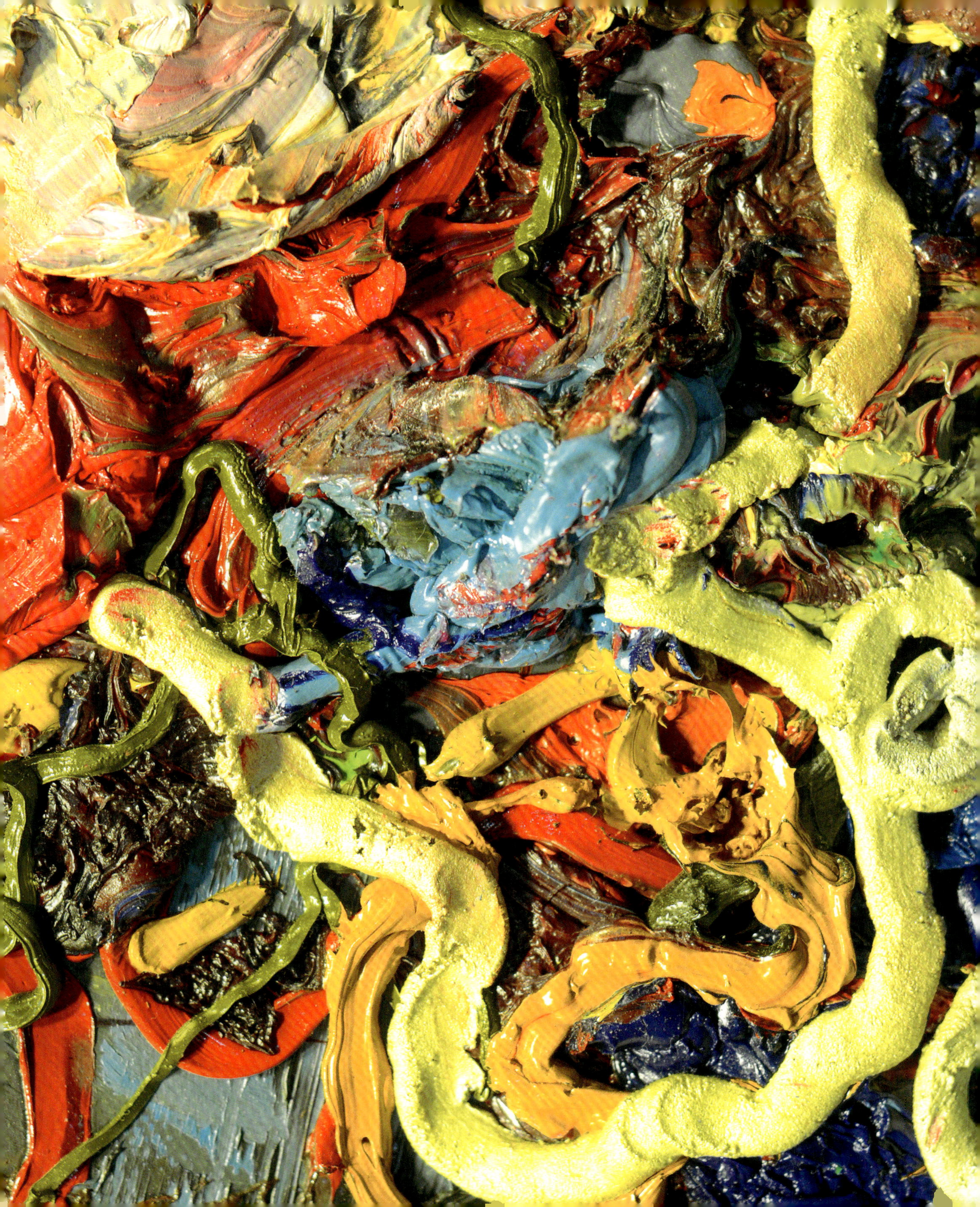

DISTANZ

JIGGER CRUZ

4 *Damn! For a Poor Flesh 1* and *2*, 2012

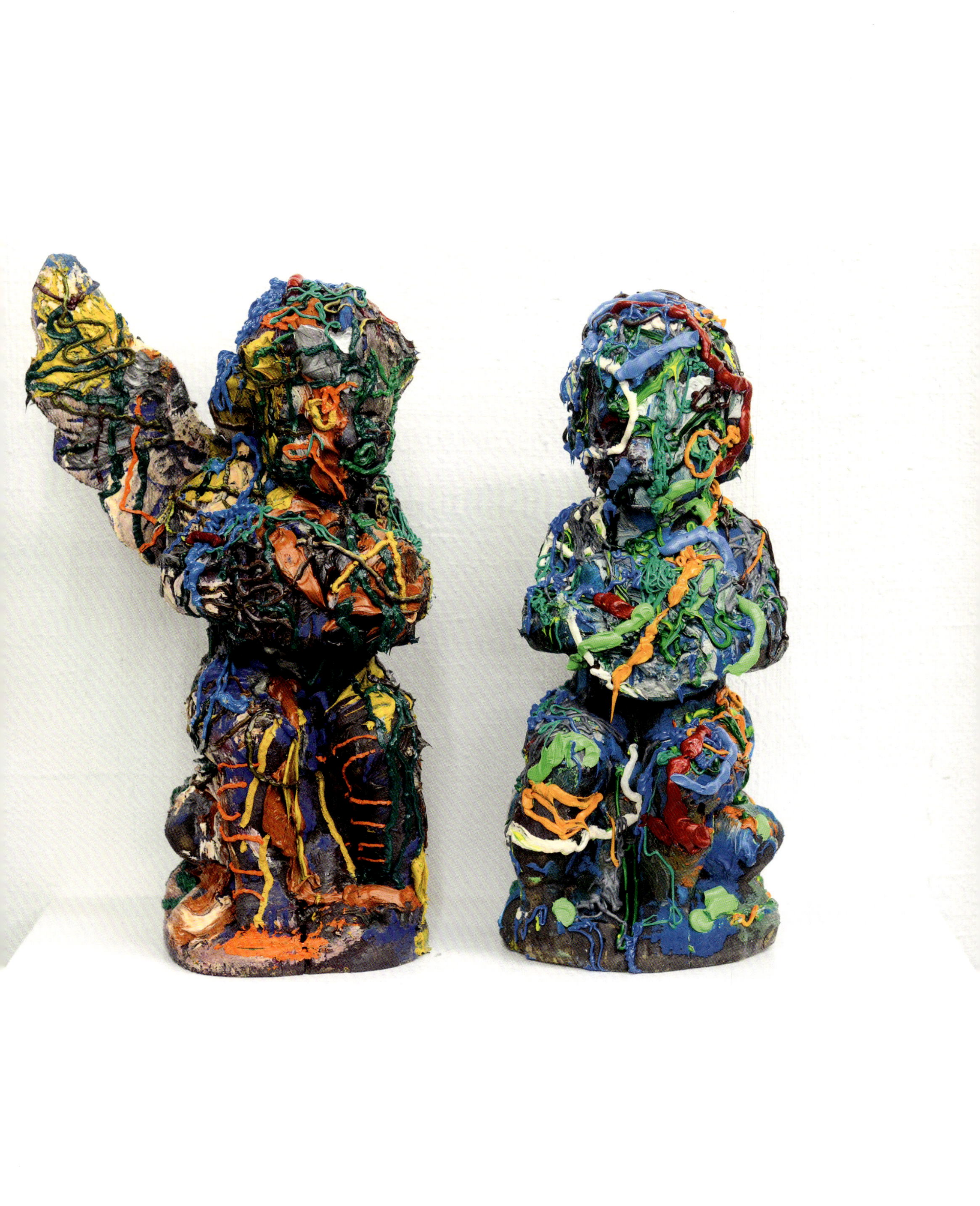

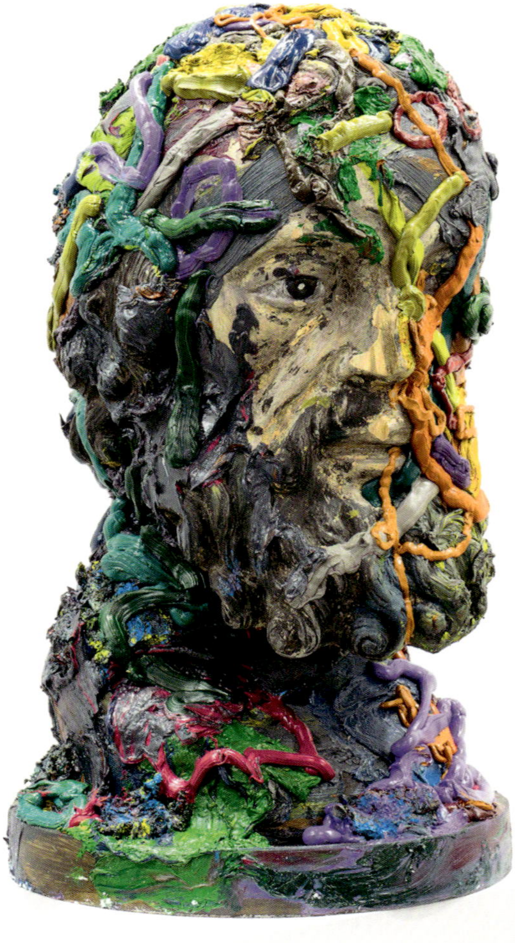

 Tracing Mental Paradise, 2014

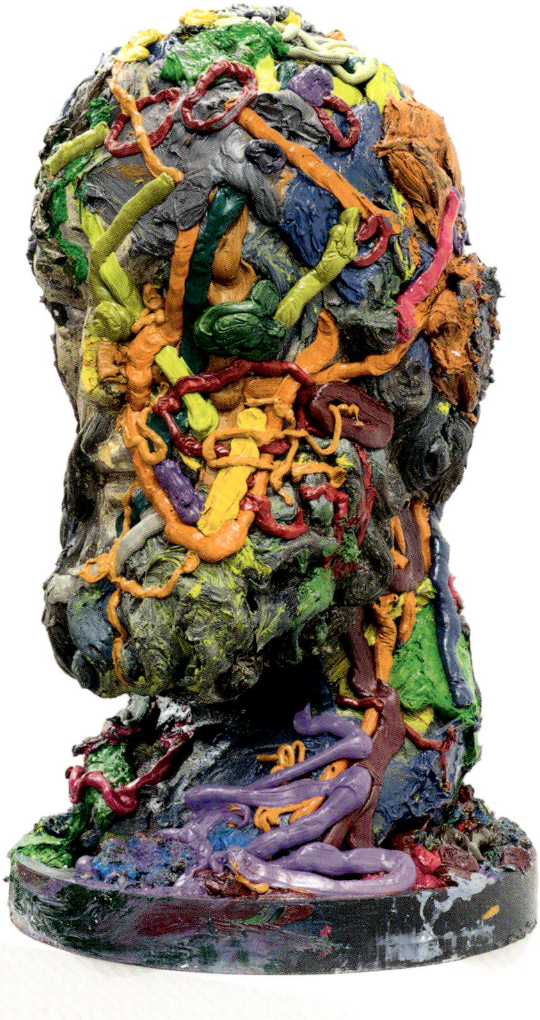

Crawling from the Wreckage, 2015

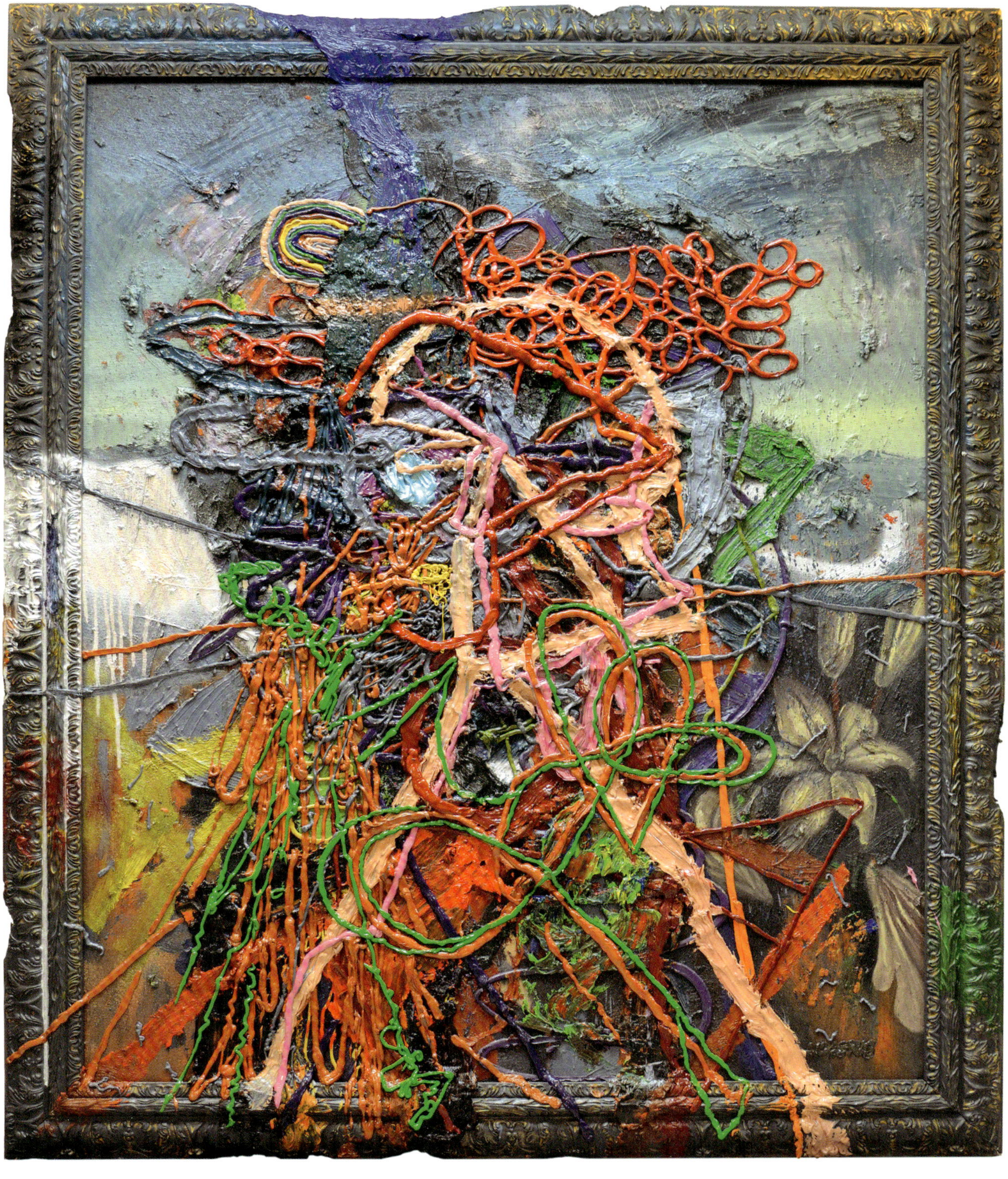

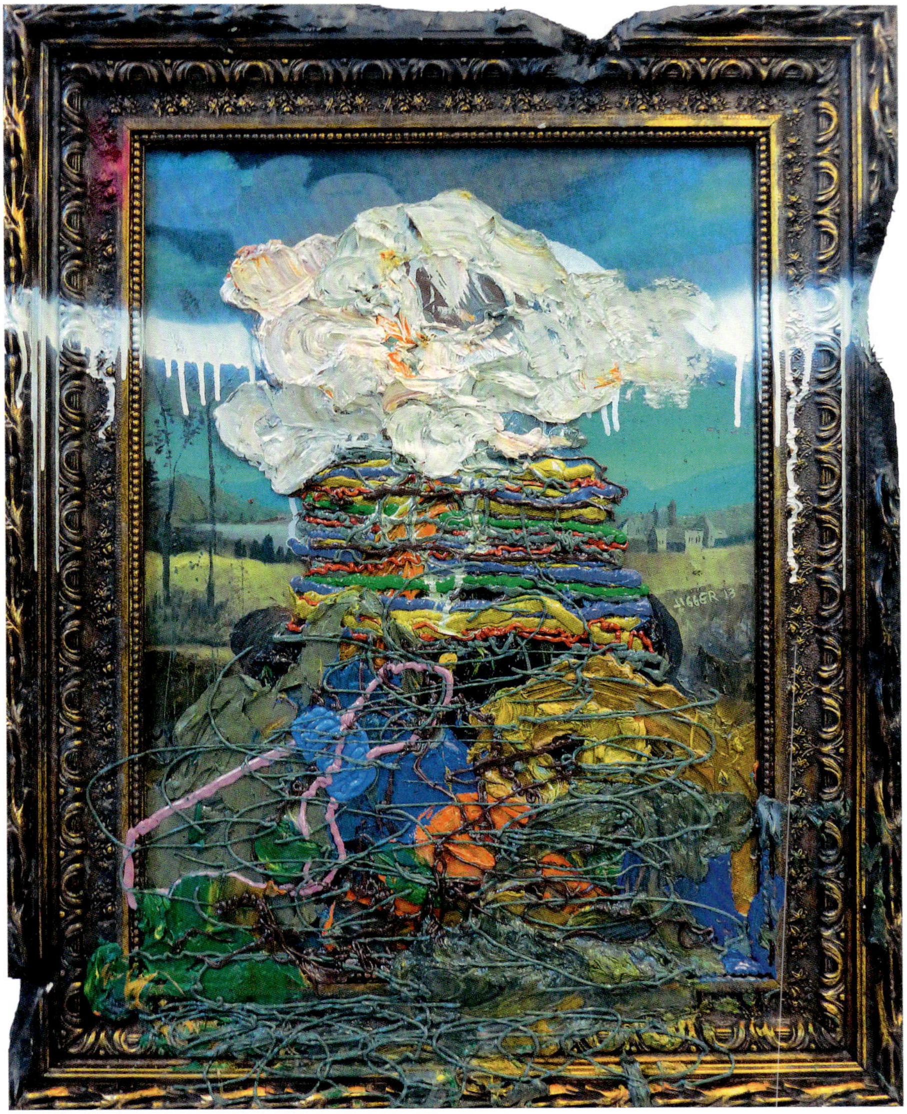

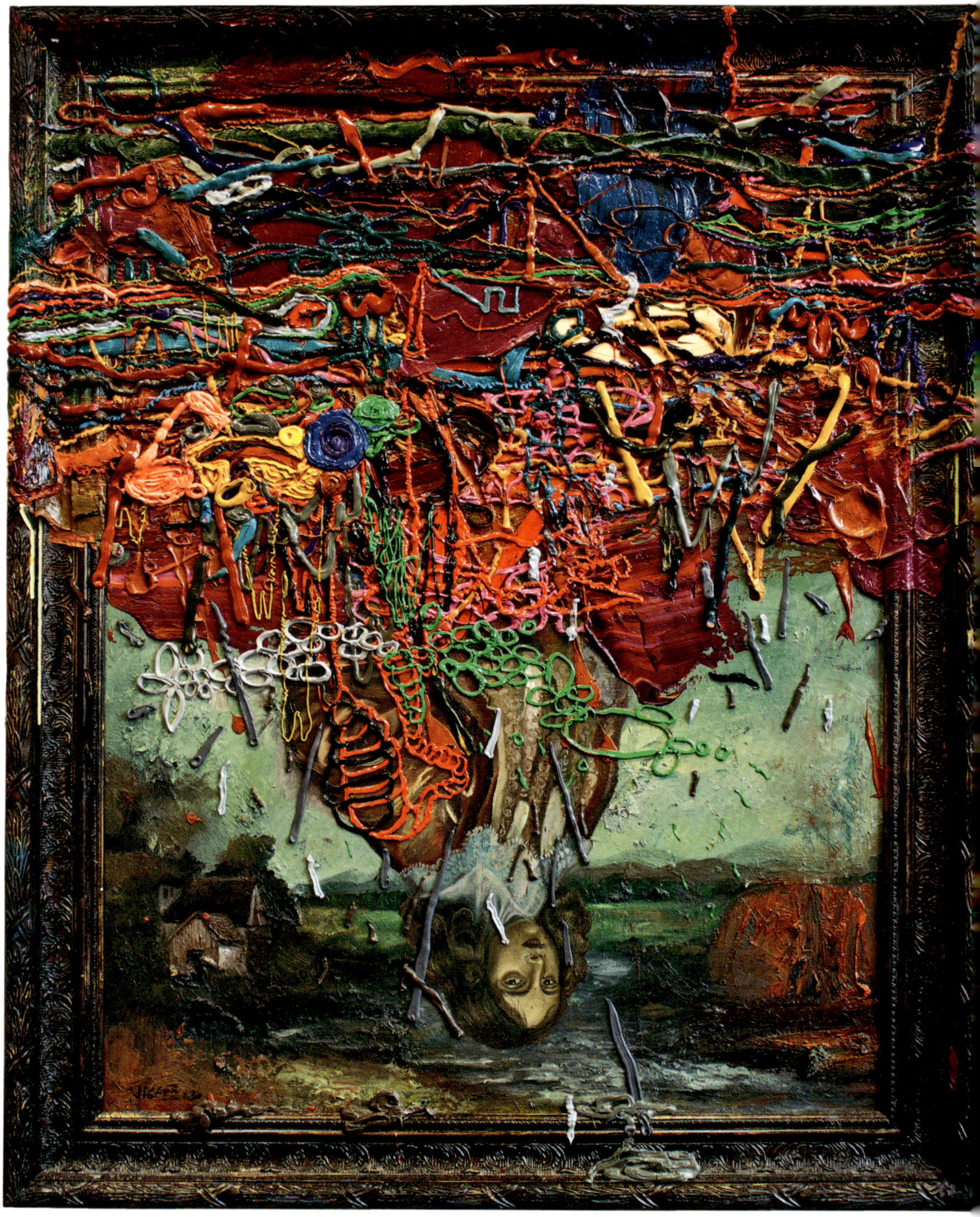

 Remix 1 and *2*, 2012

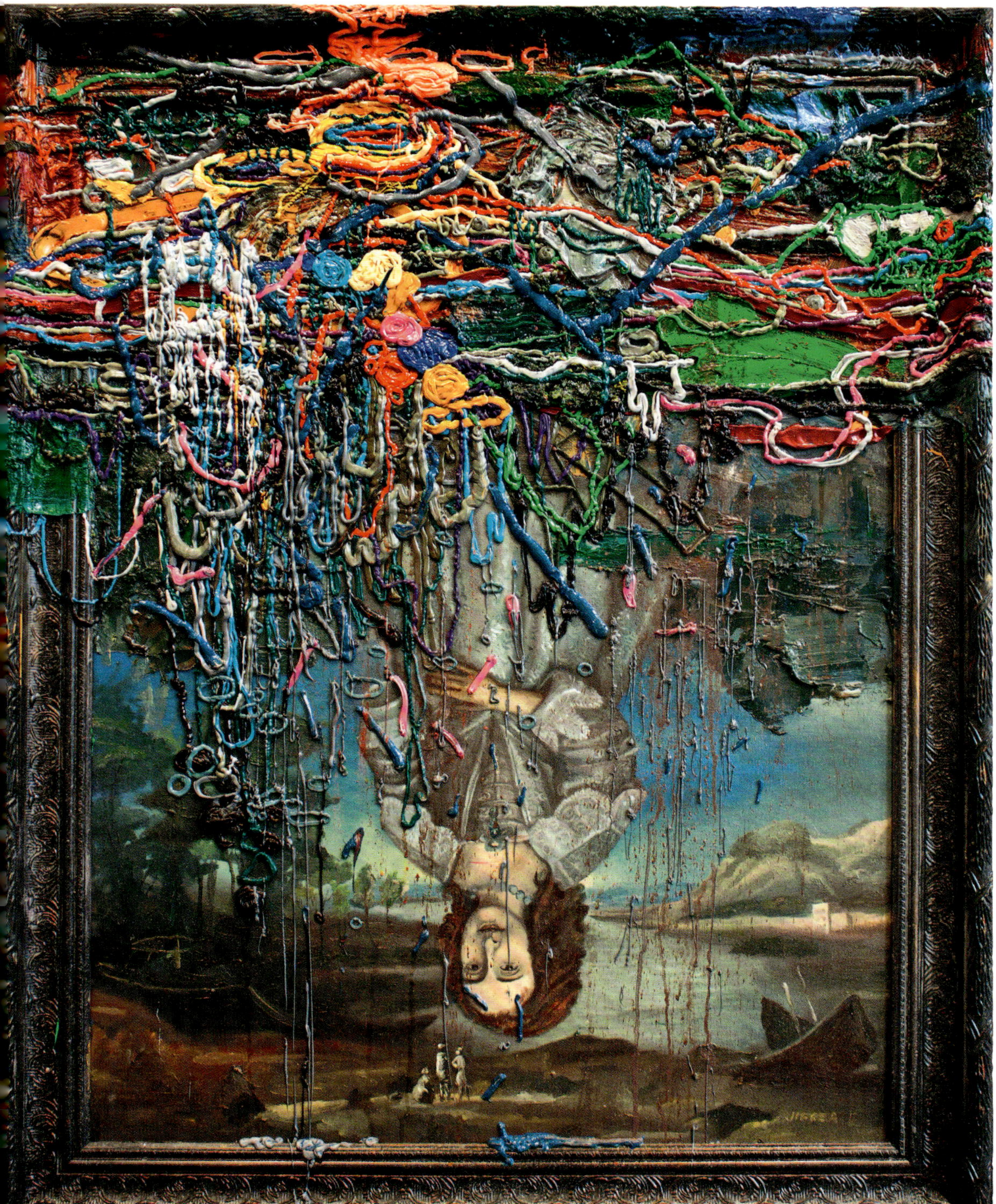

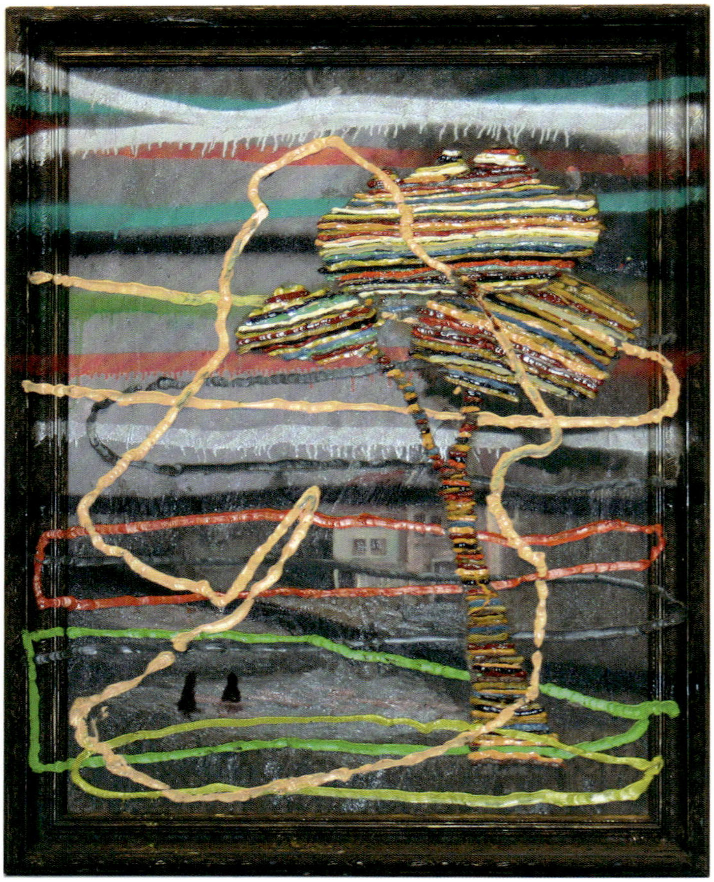

 In the Landscape of Contradictions, 2012

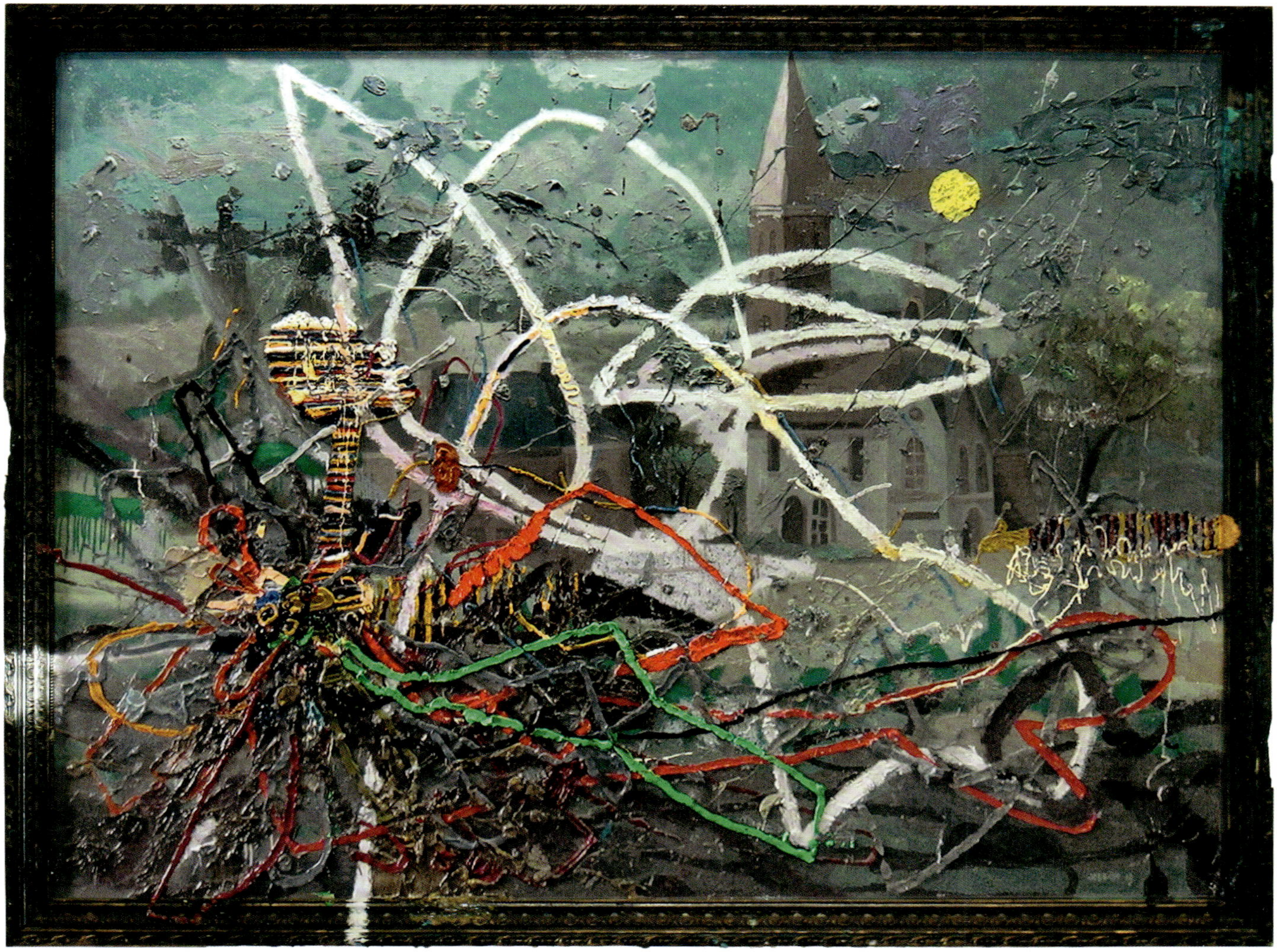

Come Like Spoiled Bells in Sudden Wind and High, 2011

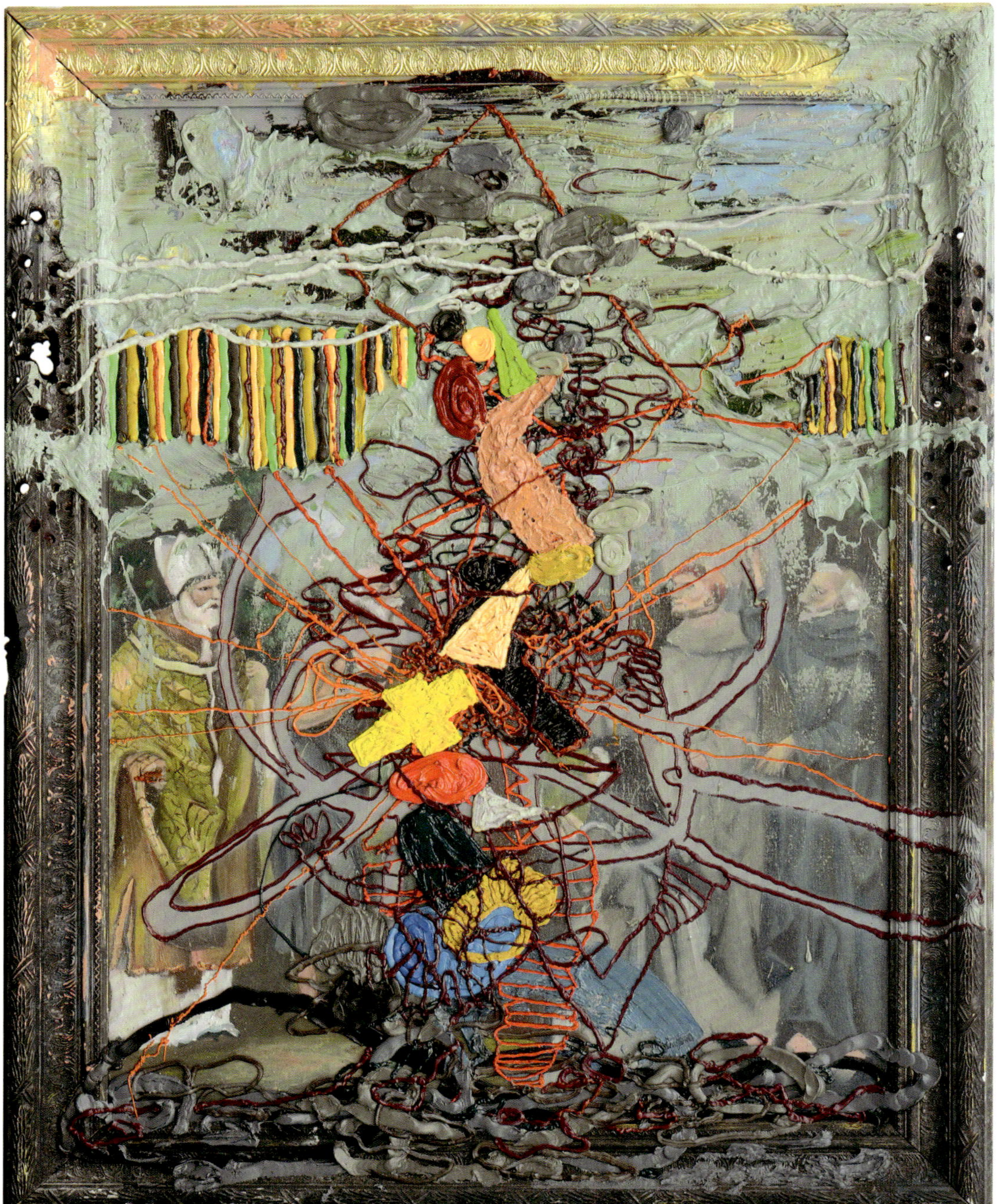

 Mystification of the False Truth, 2012

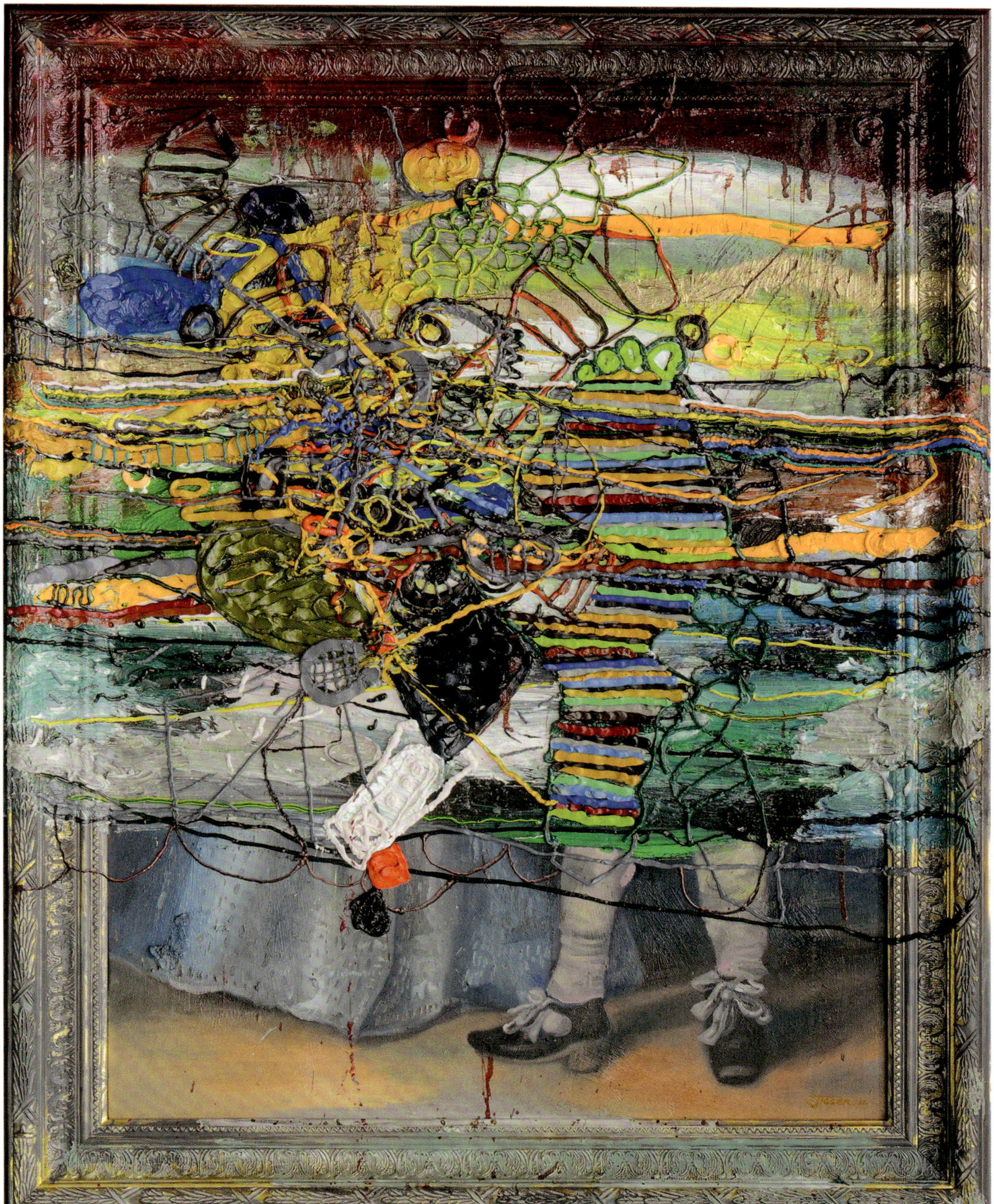

Finitudes Against the Distortion, 2012

A Pause in the Triumph of Existence, 2013

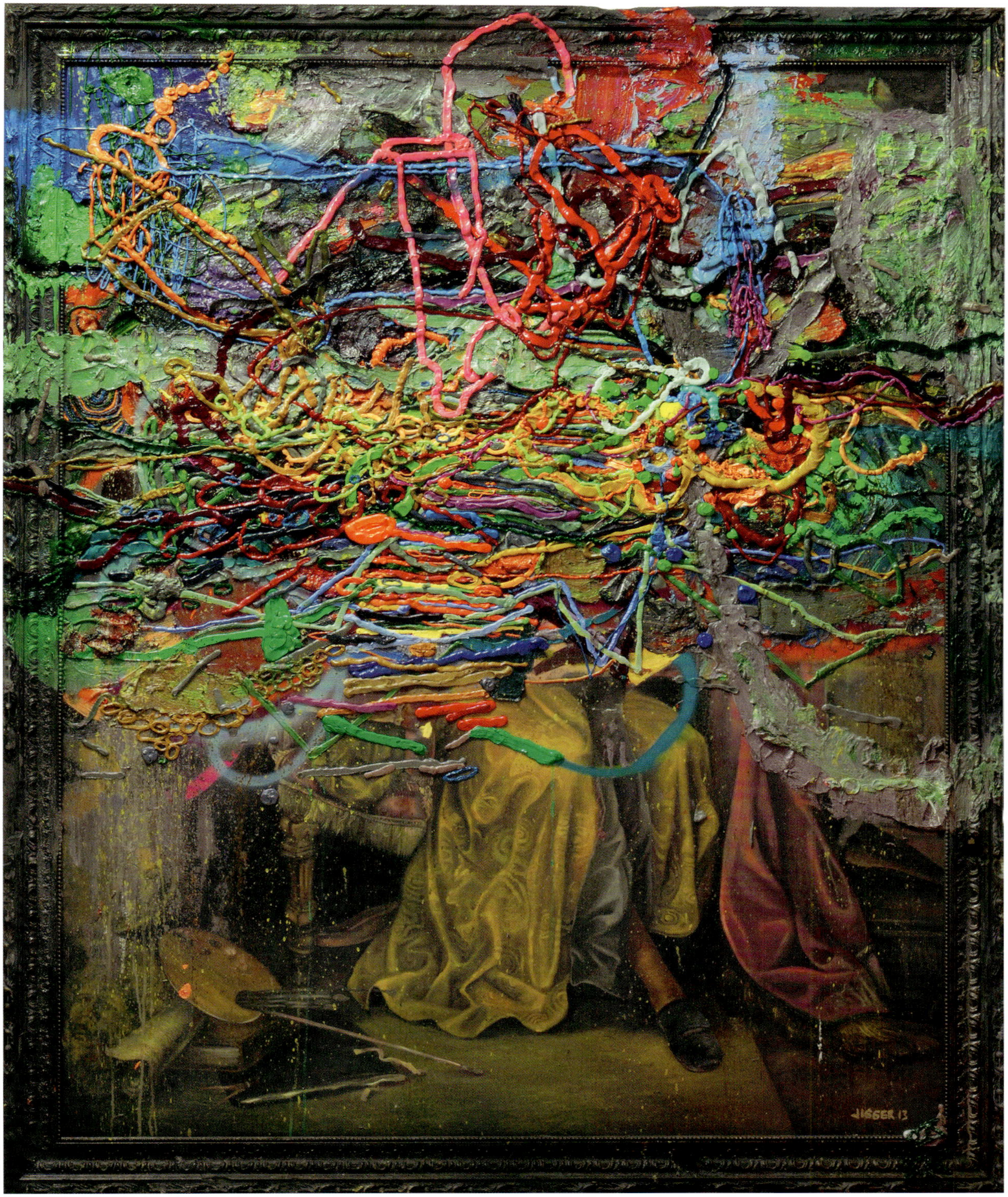

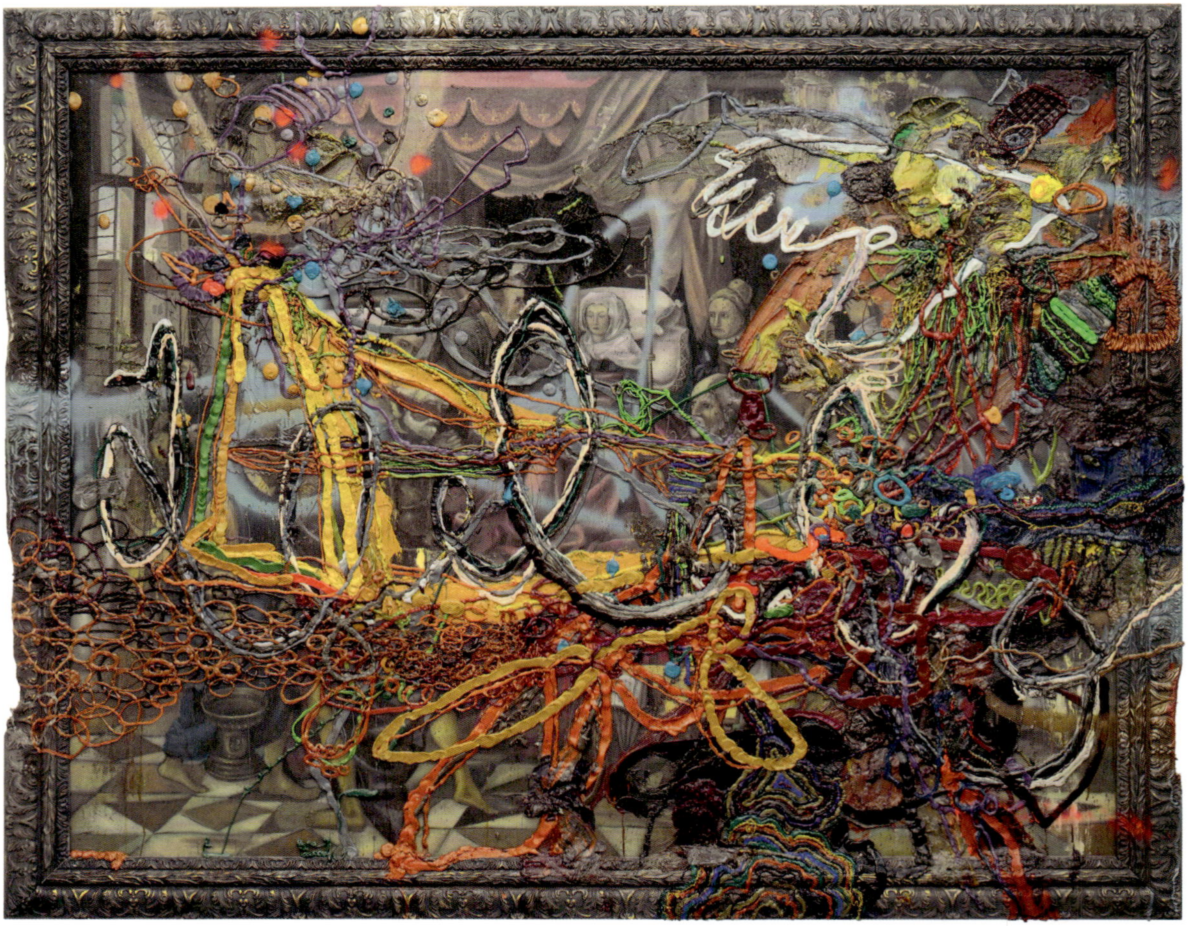

 Blares of the Opposite, 2013

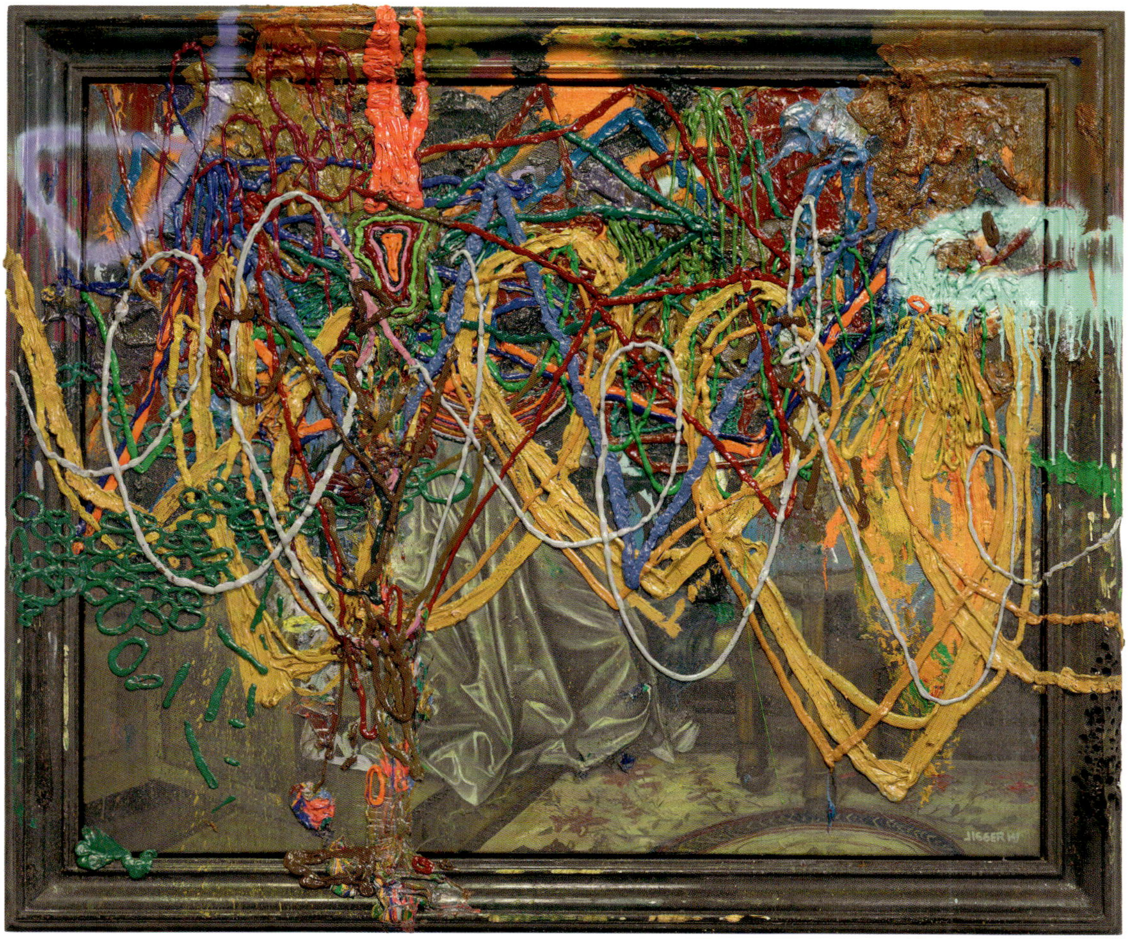

Platforms of Dispositional Overtone, 2014

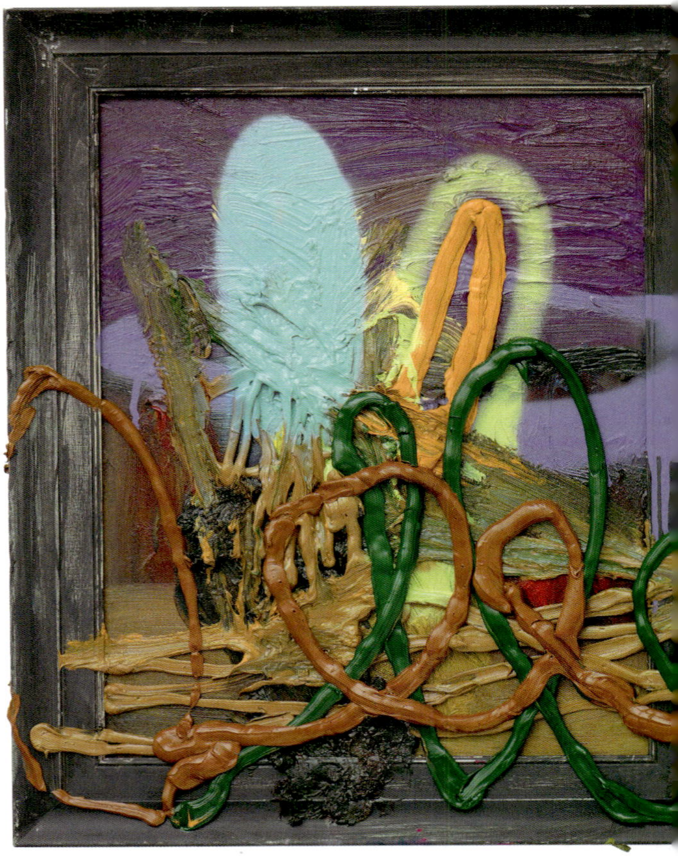

 Between Planes and Parallels, 2014

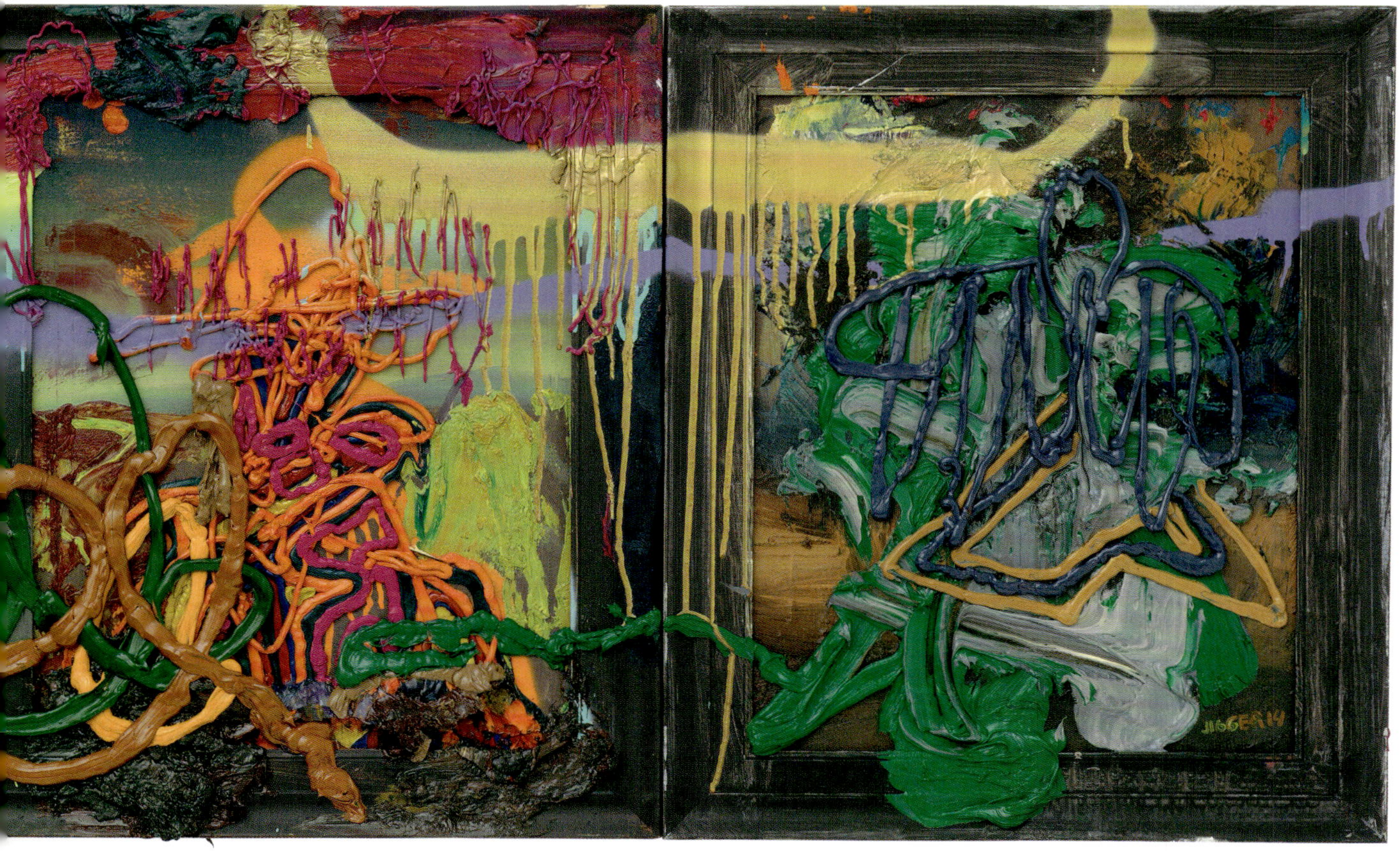

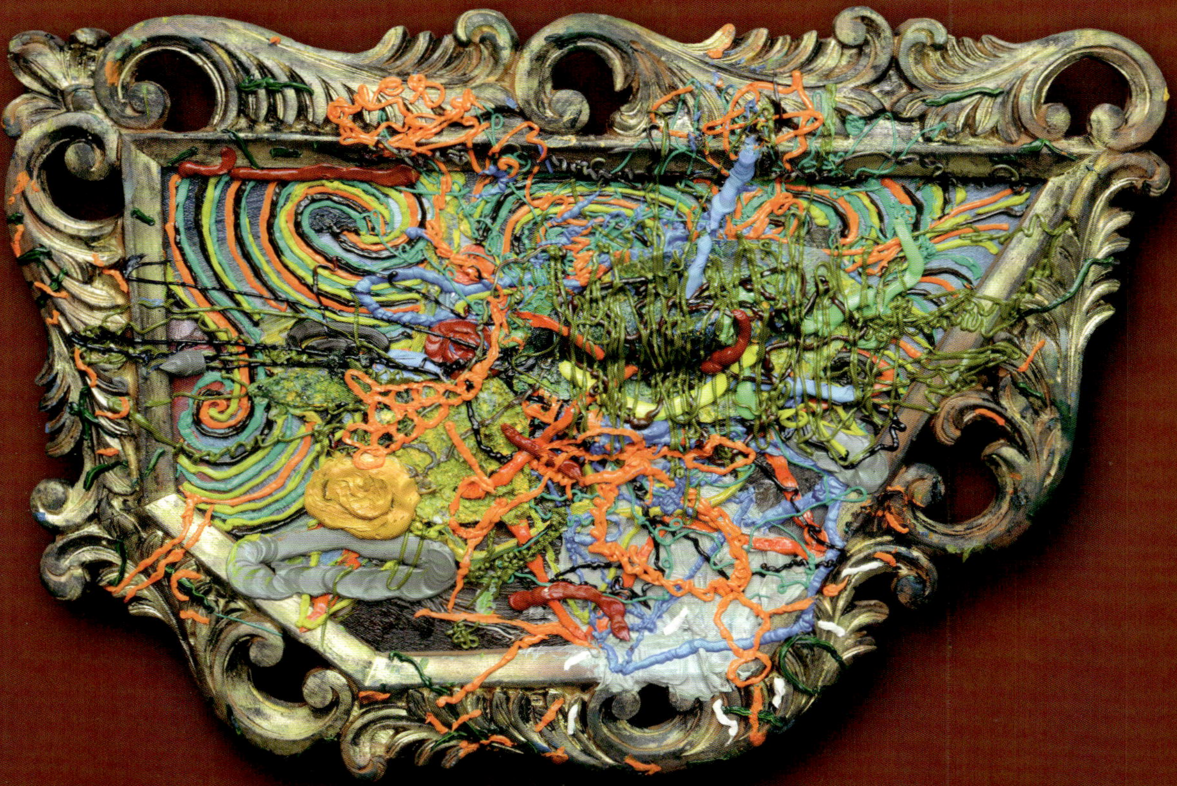

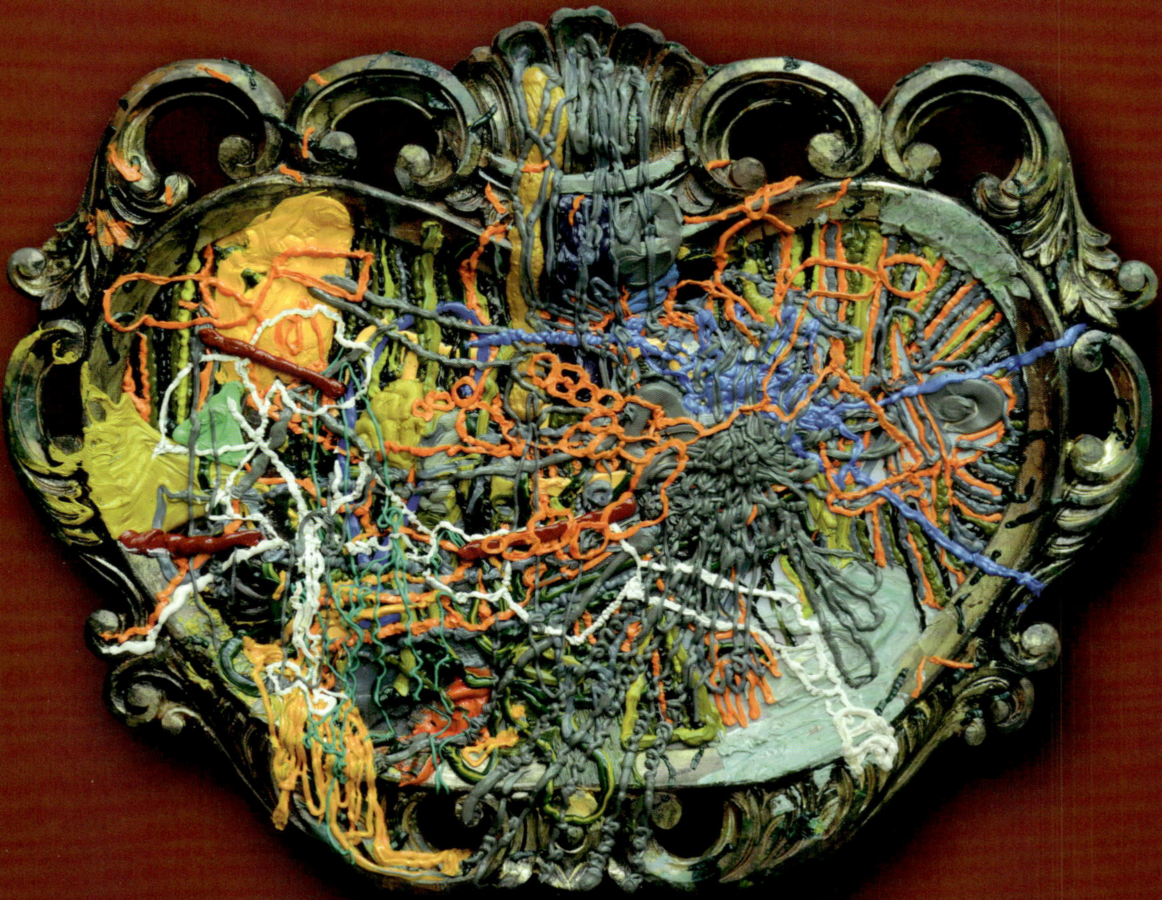

 Embrace of the Duchampian Impulse 2, 2012

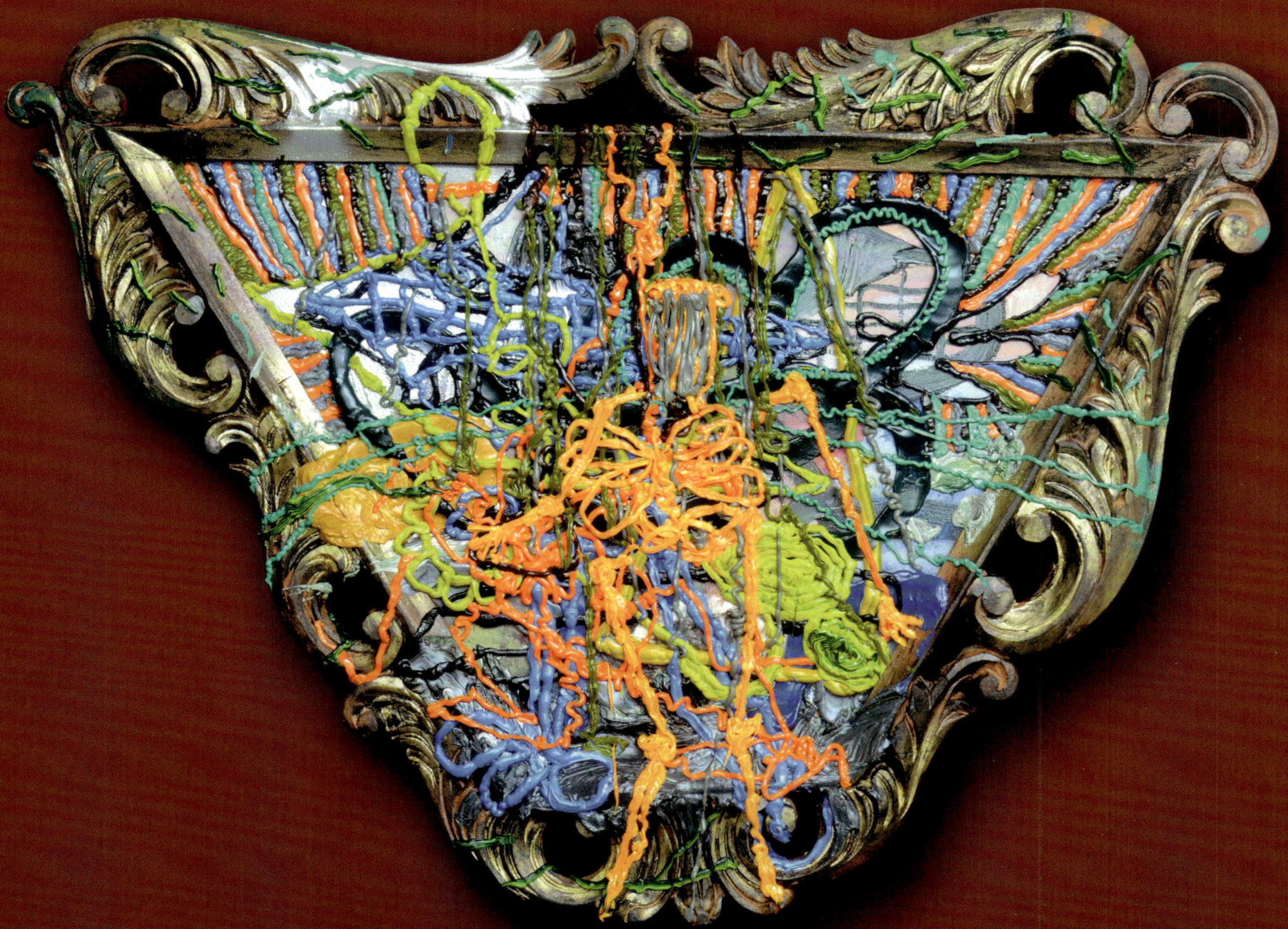

Embrace of the Duchampian Impulse 1, 2012

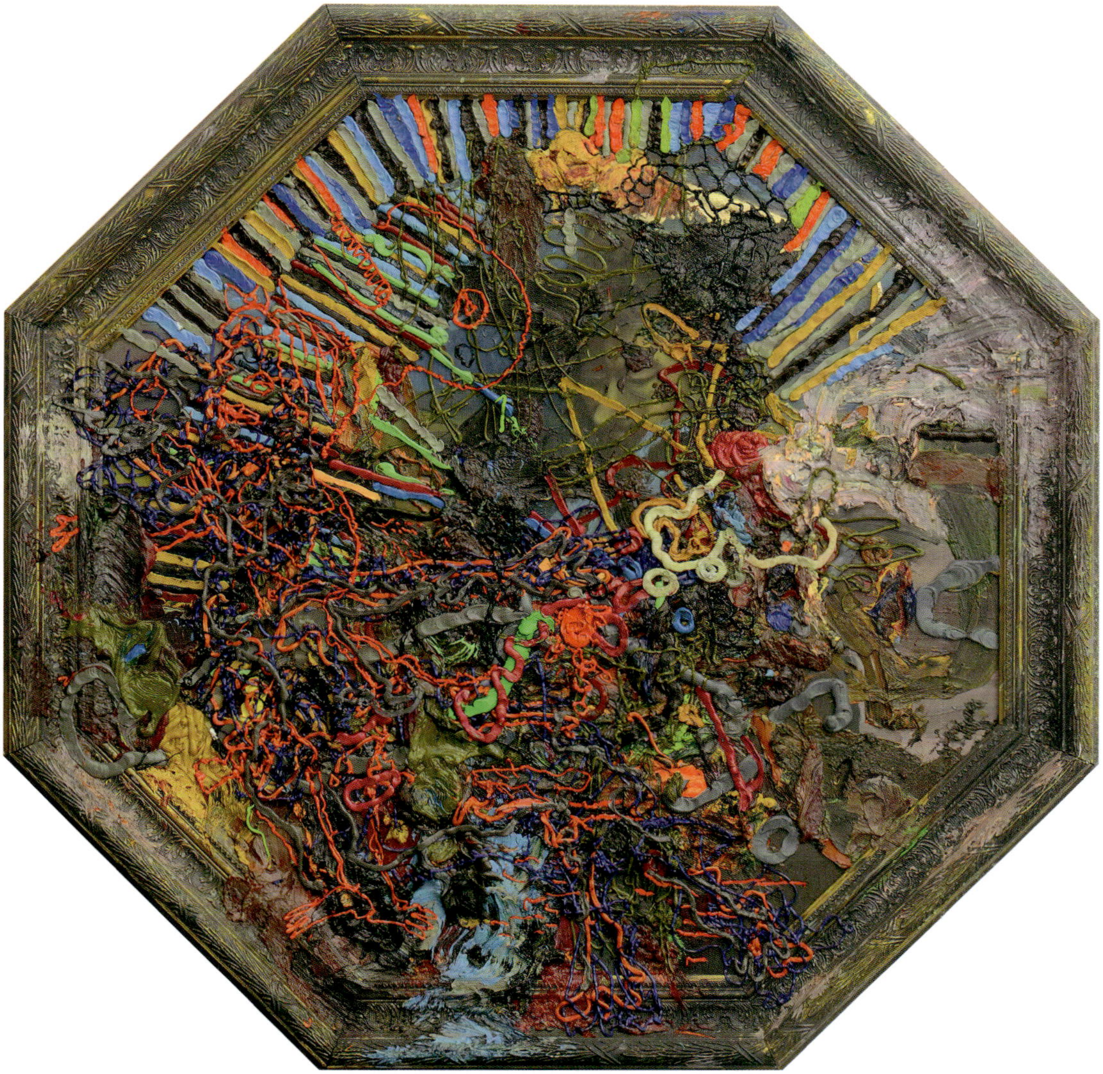

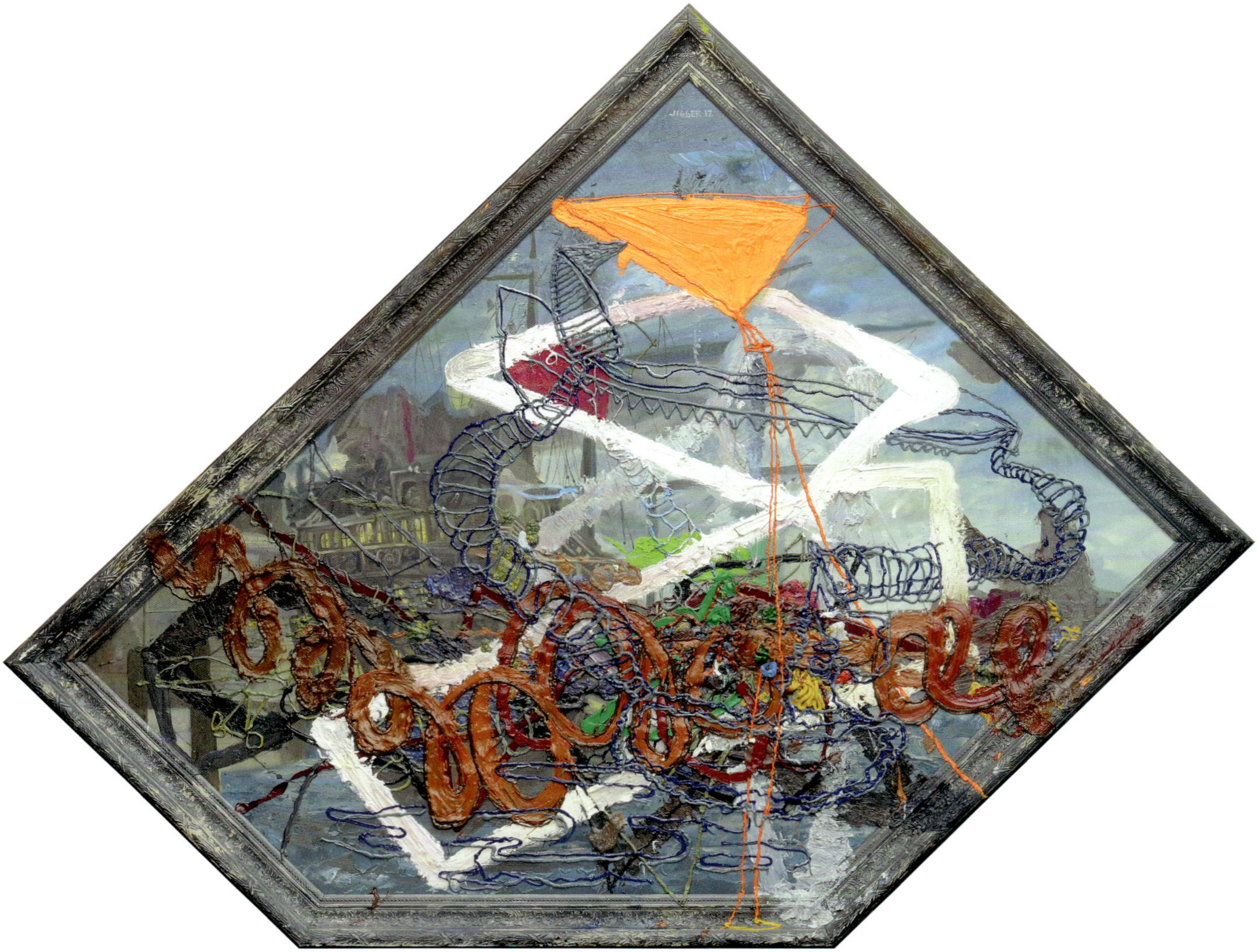

The Ballad of Representational World, 2012

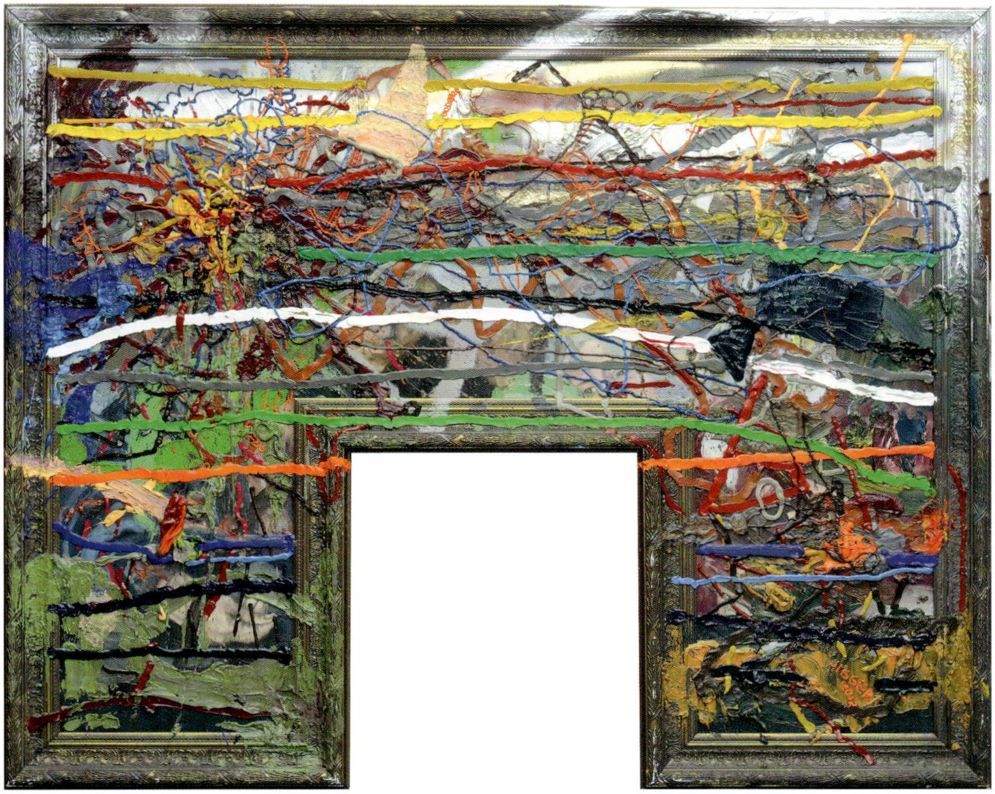

Spatial Soother, 2012

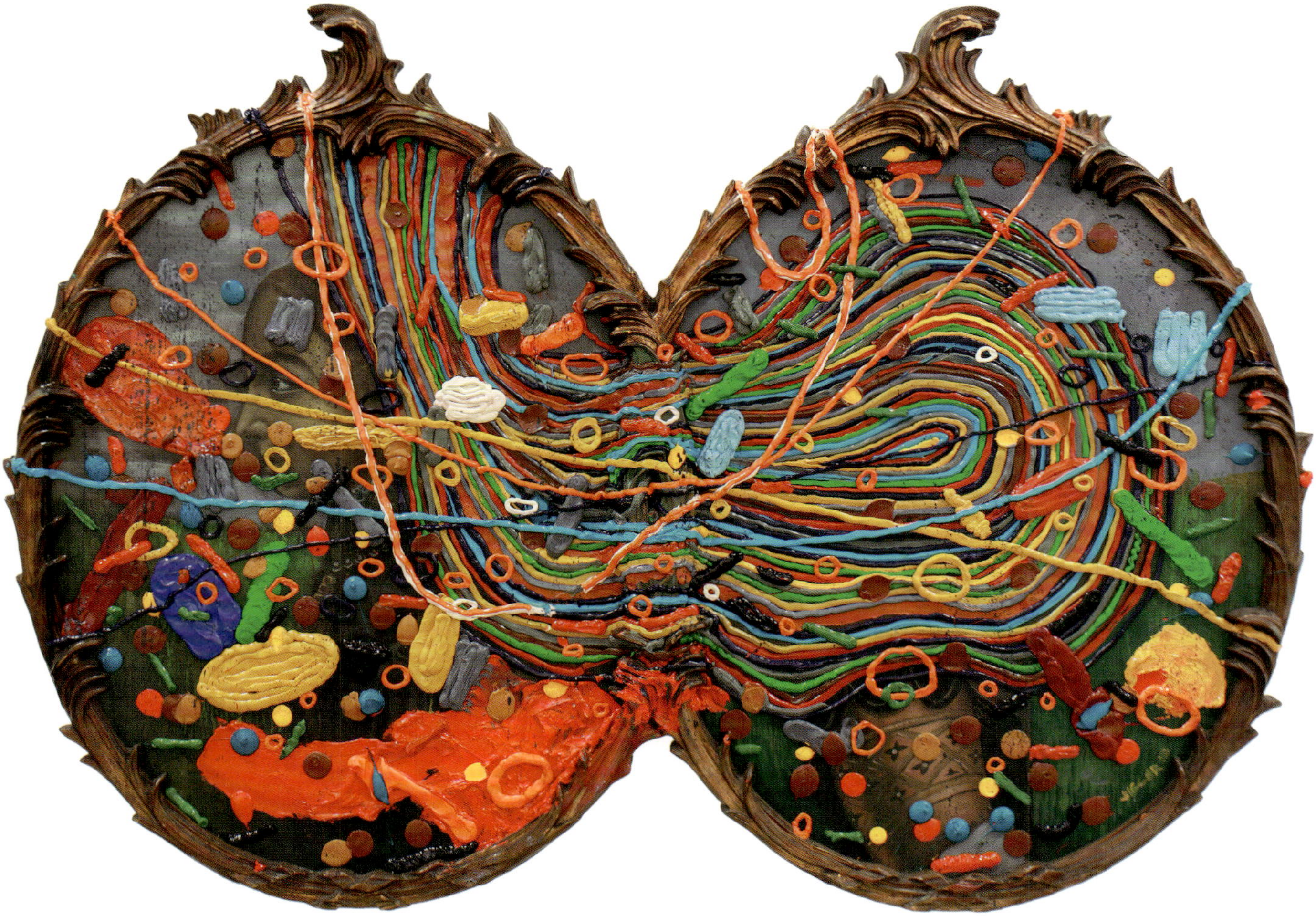

Saints in a Monumental Displacement, 2013

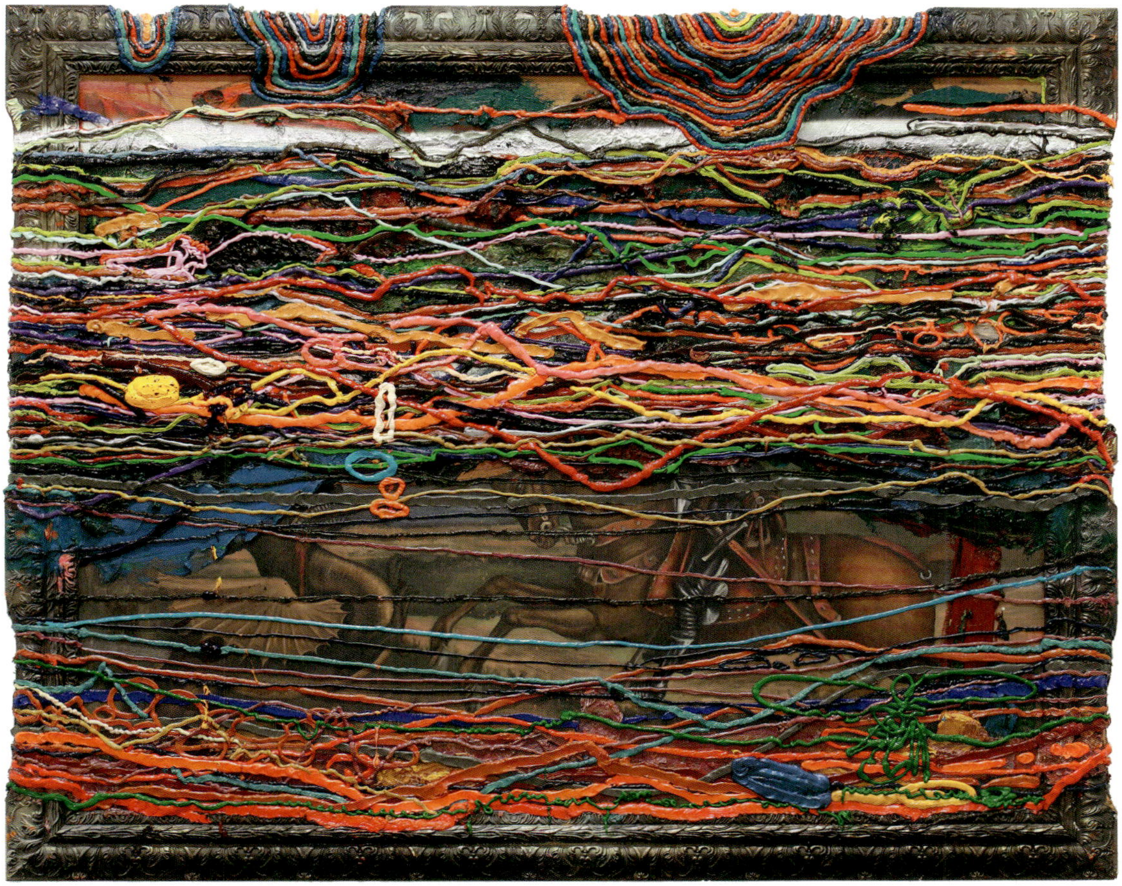

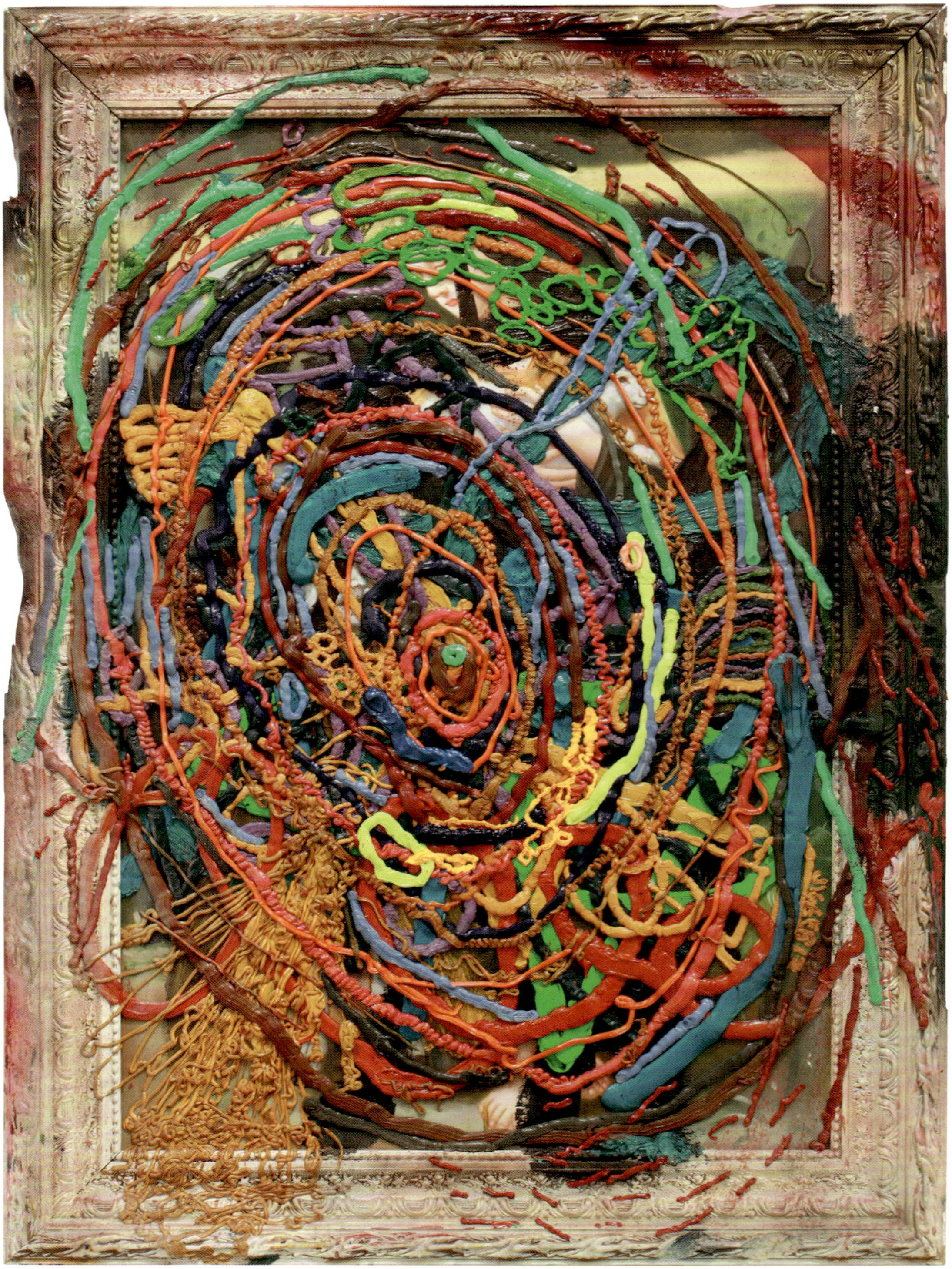

 Orbit, 2013

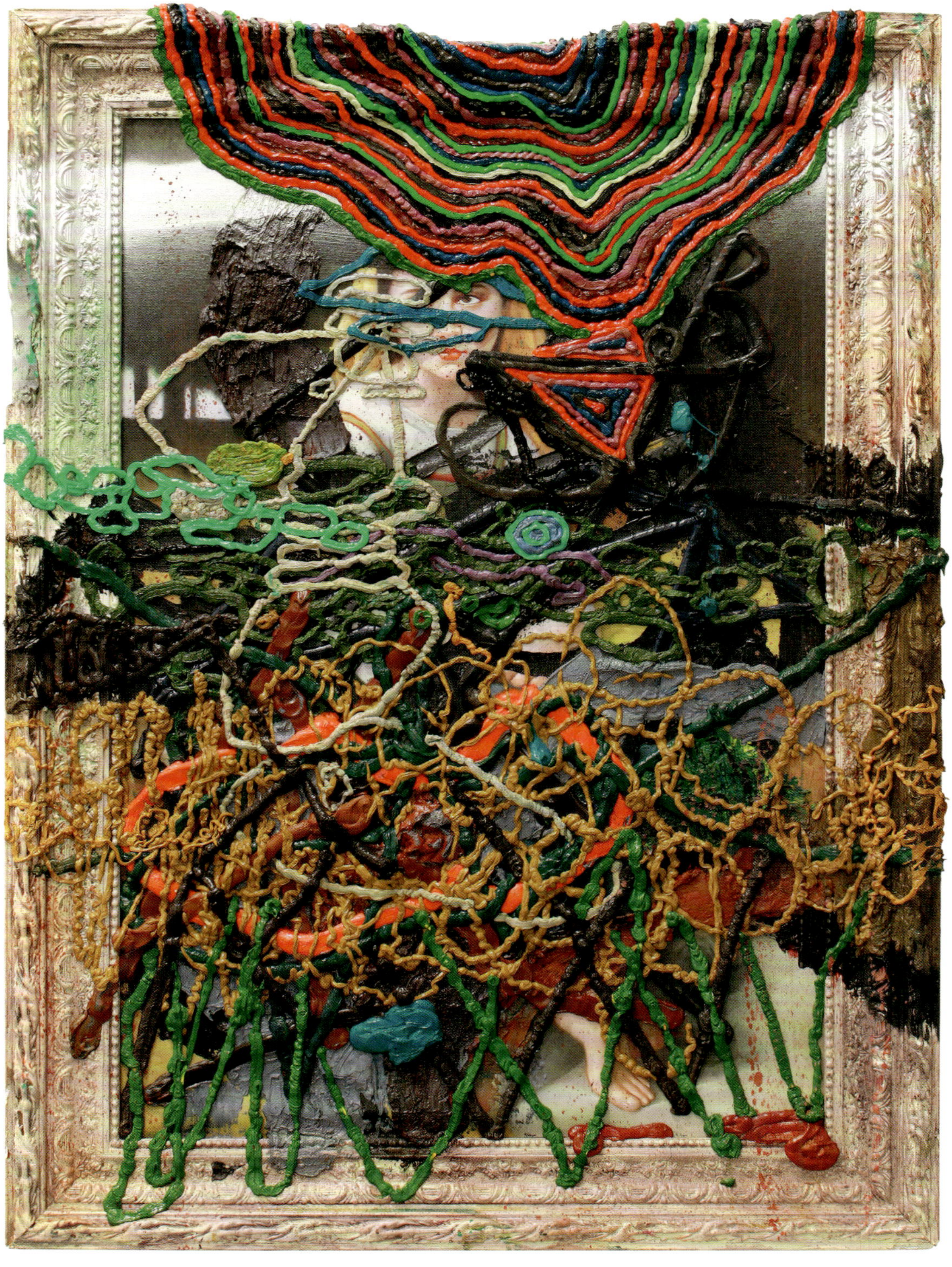

An Awful Ruin behind the Melting Sunrise, 2013

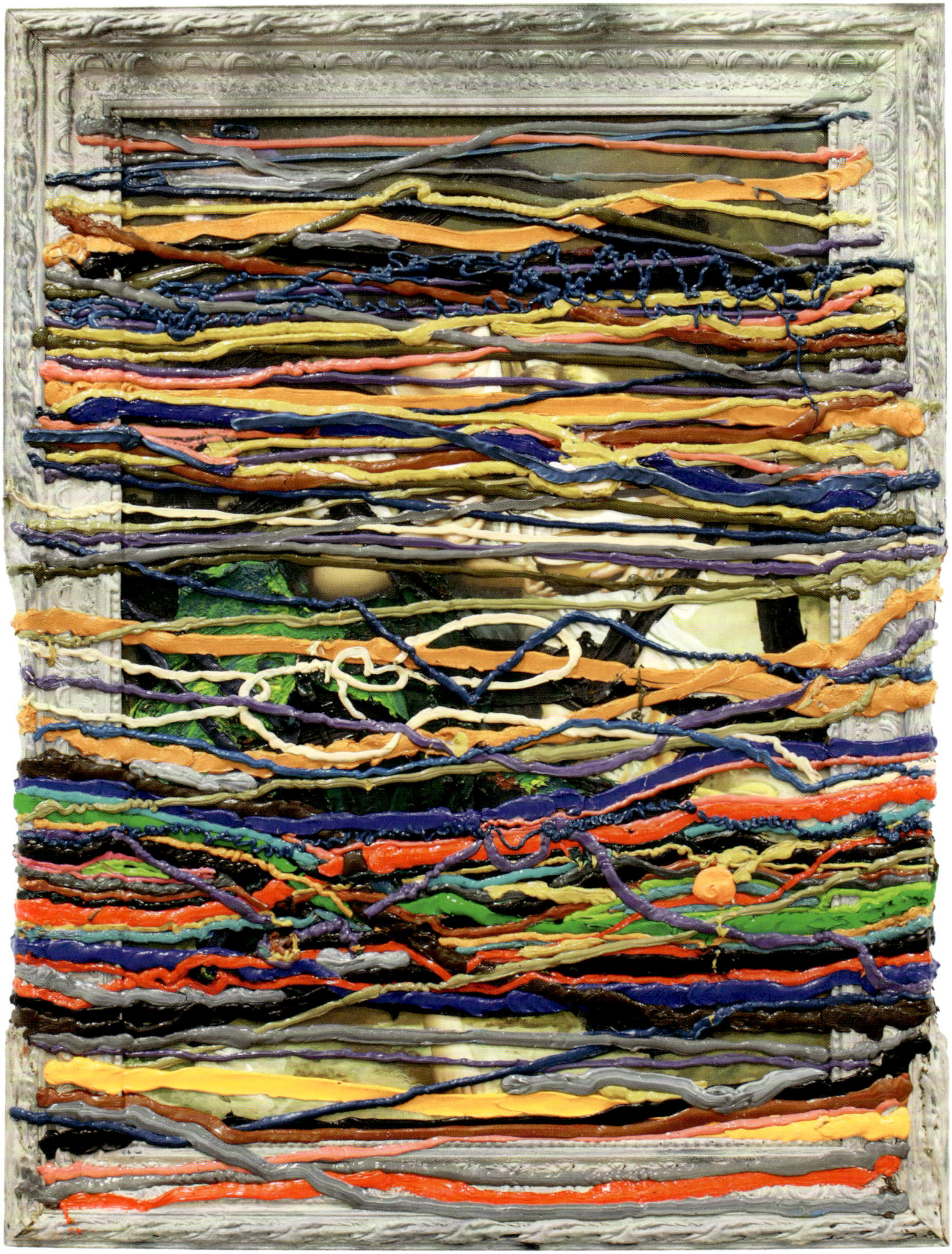

Horizontal Trap, 2013

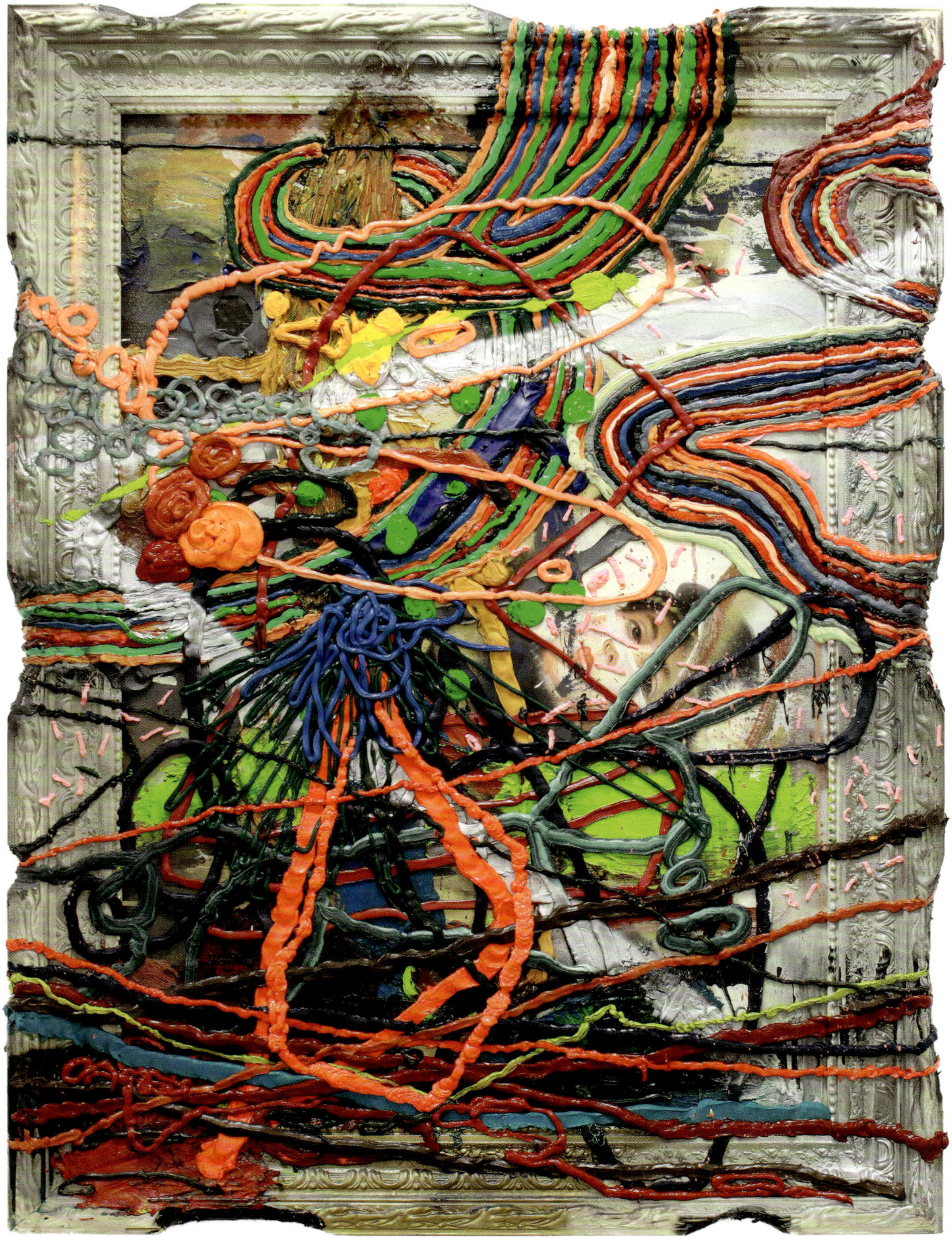

Narratives of Chromophobics, 2013

Before the Night Grows Old, 2015

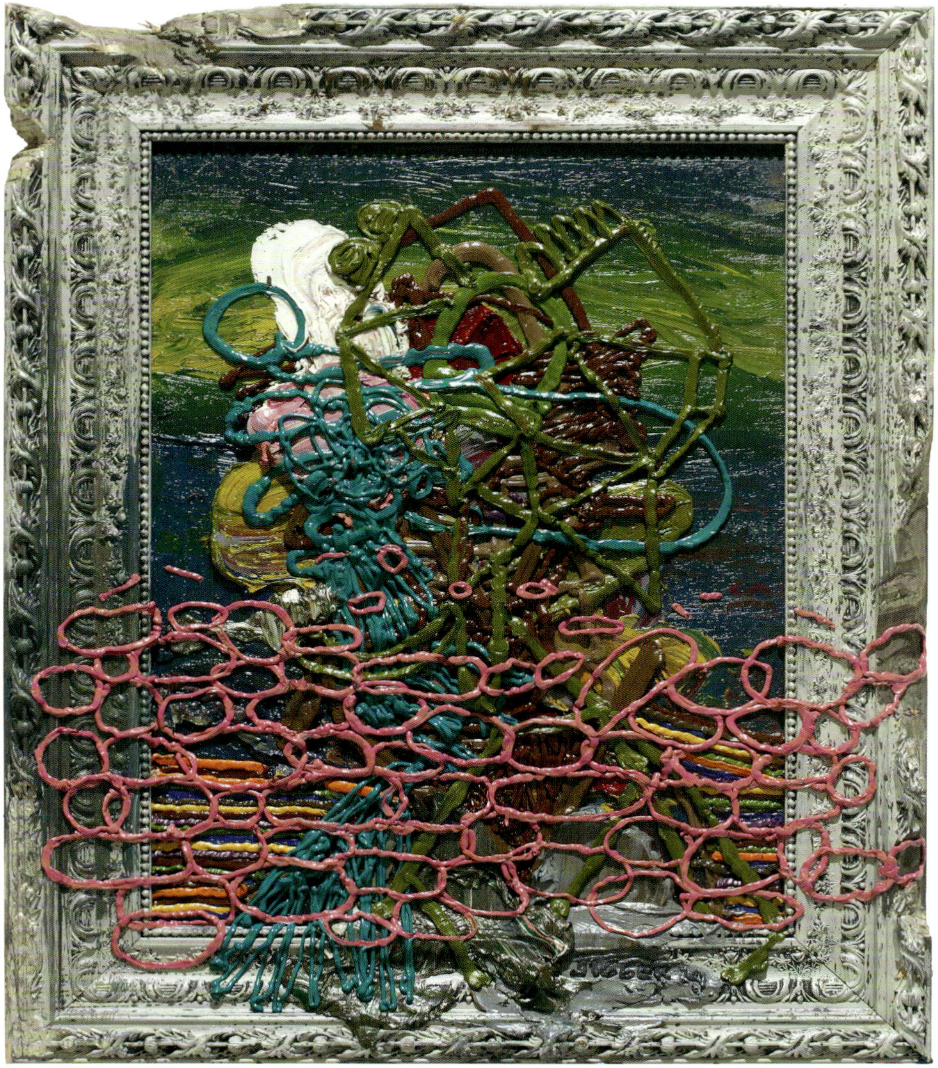

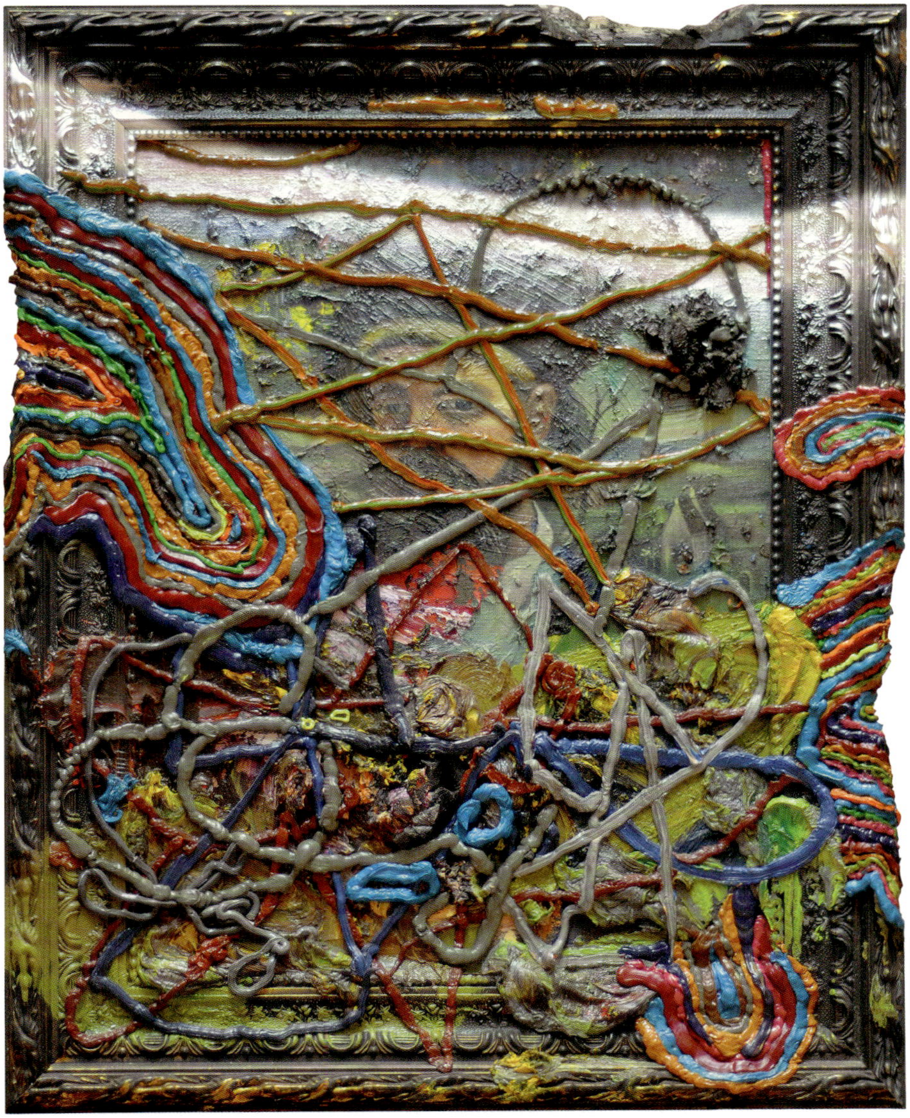

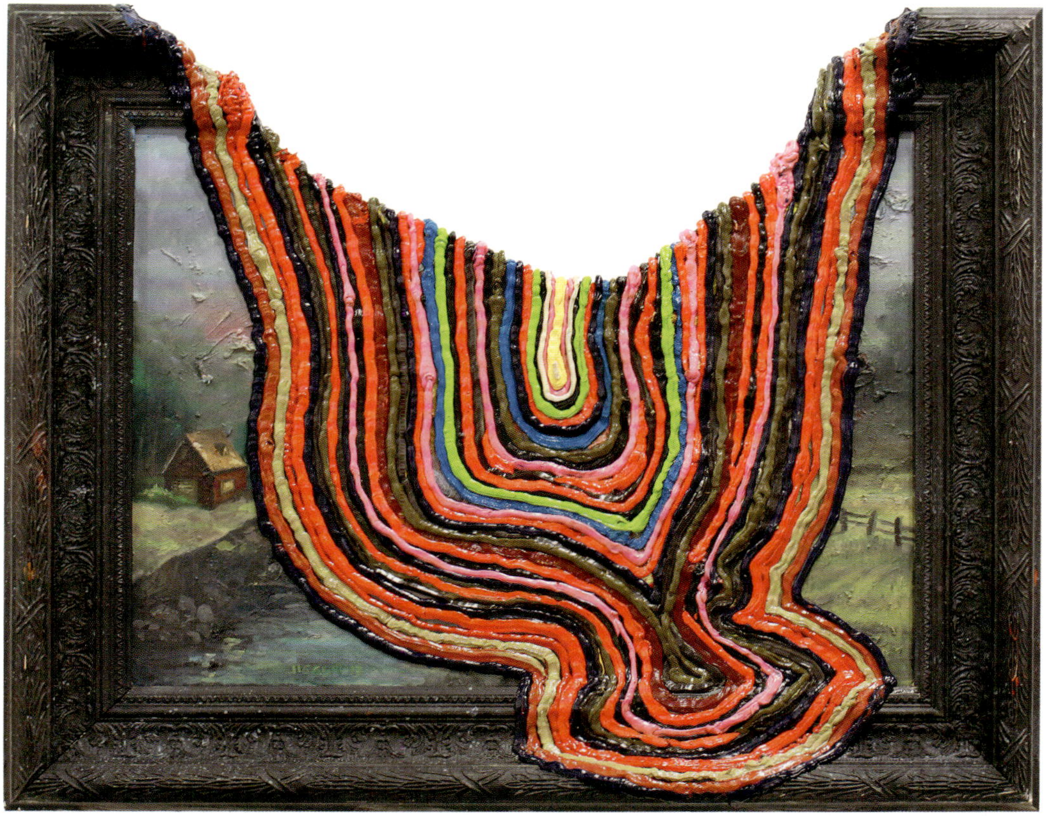

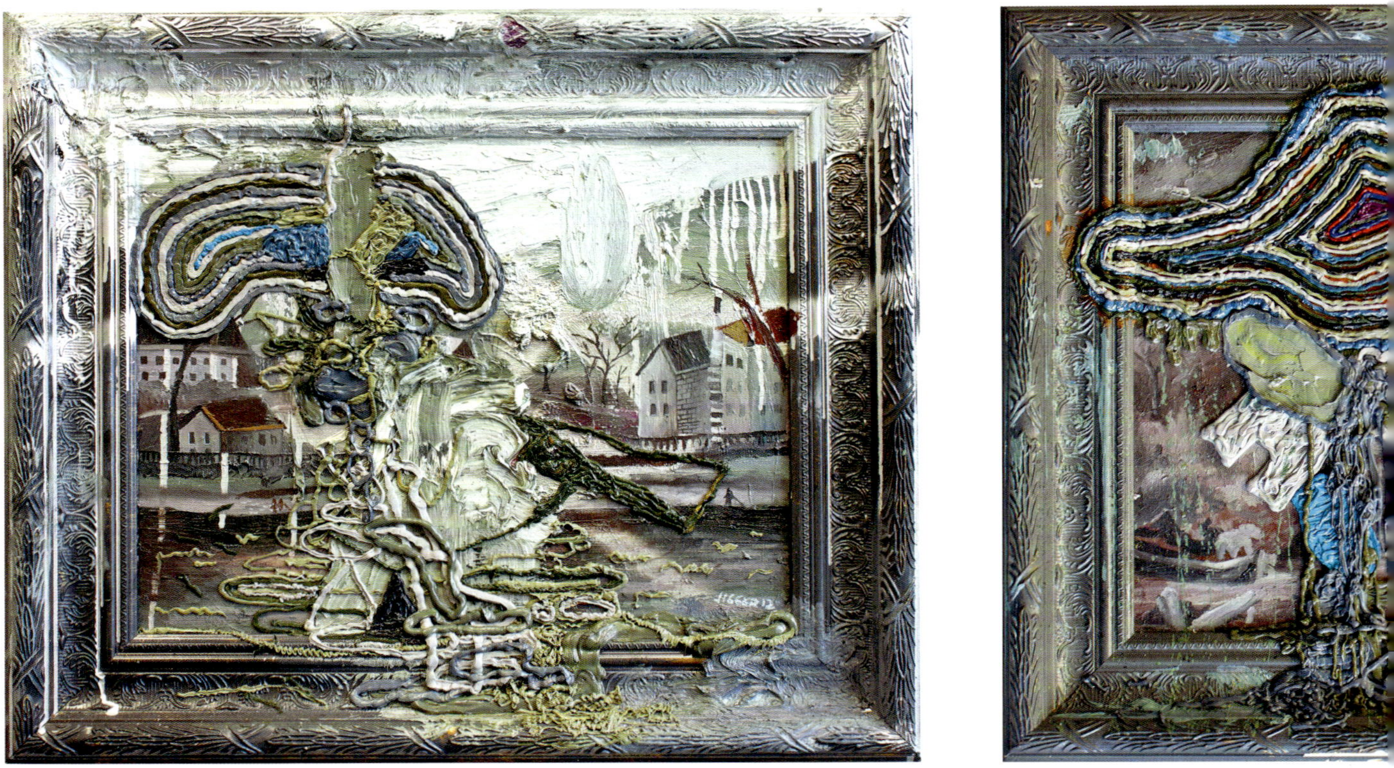

 Euphoria 1–3, 2012

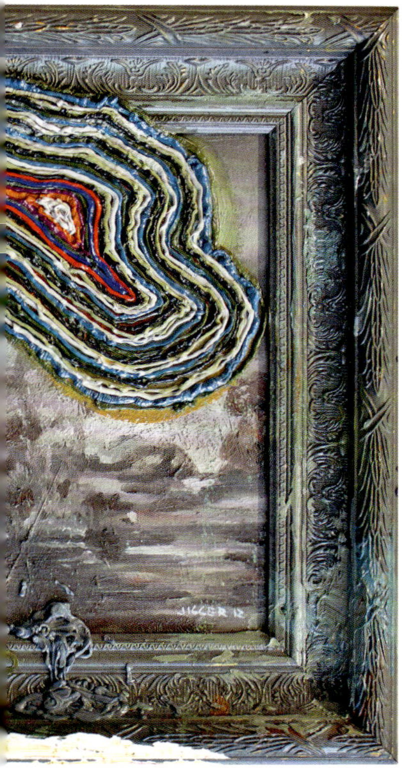
JIGGER 12

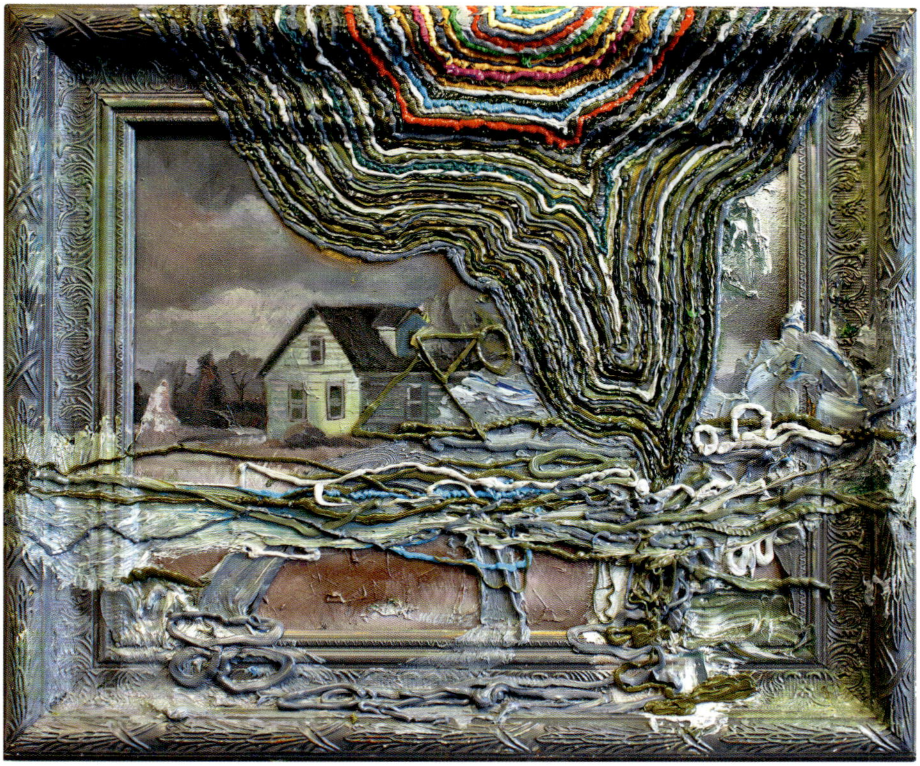

The Green, The Yellow and The Blues, 2013

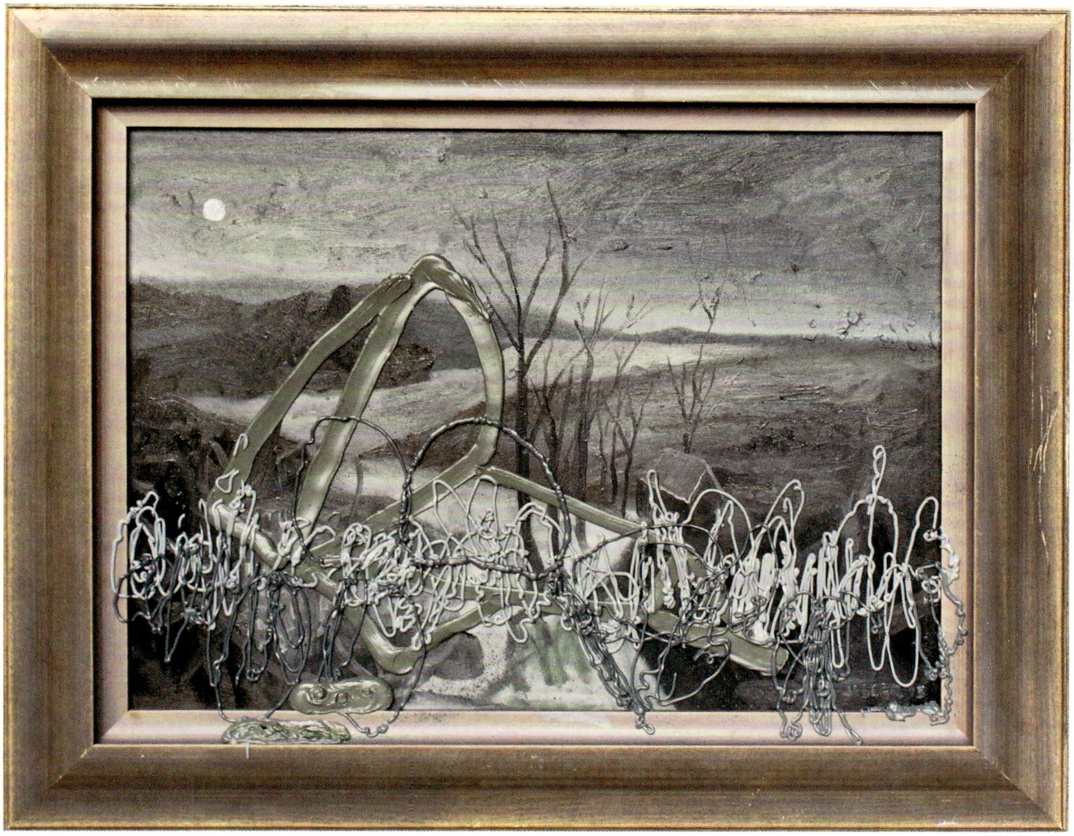

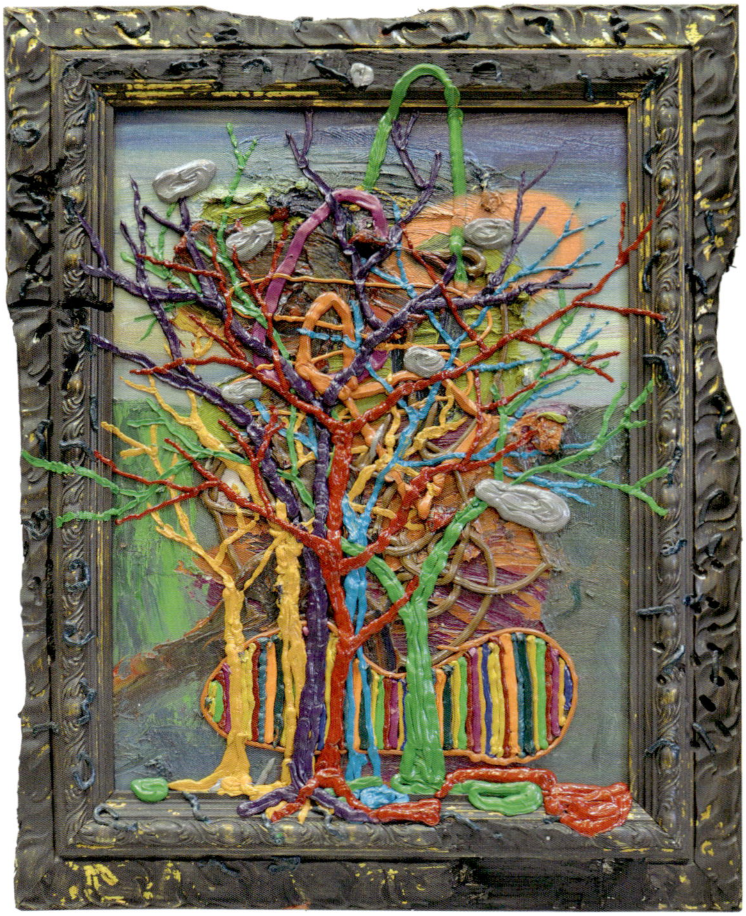

 Silent Summer, 2015

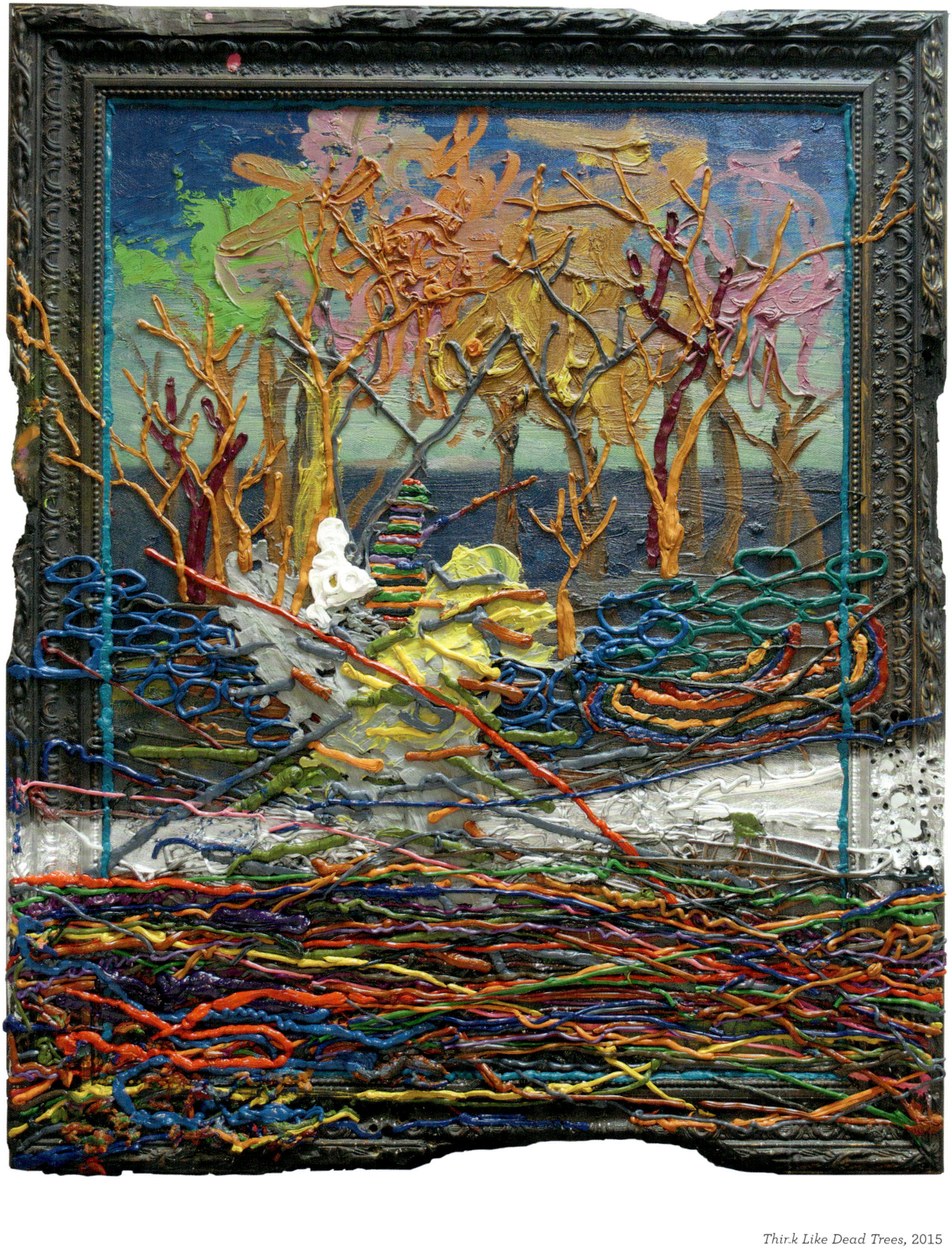

Think Like Dead Trees, 2015

 Yellows with a Little Sense of Terror, 2014

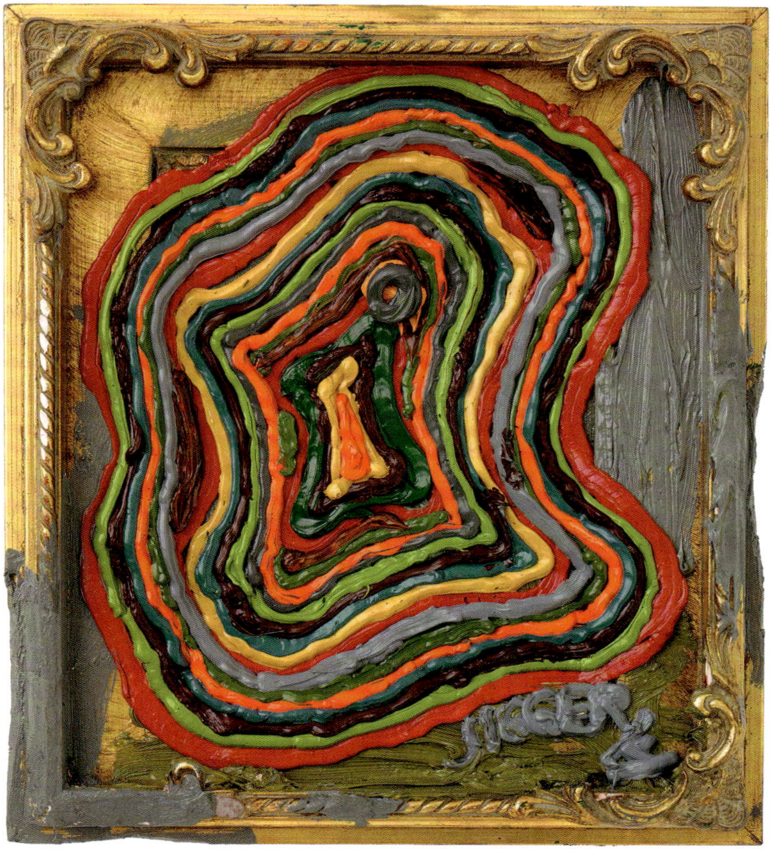

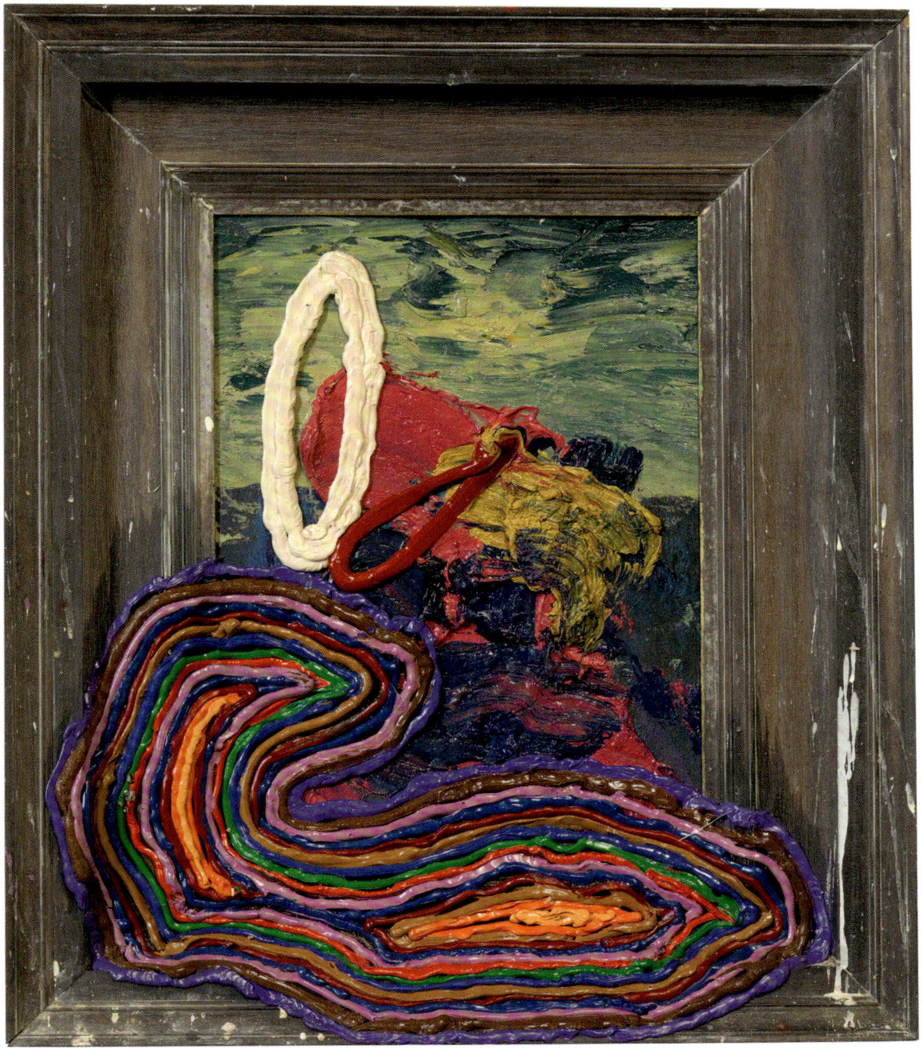

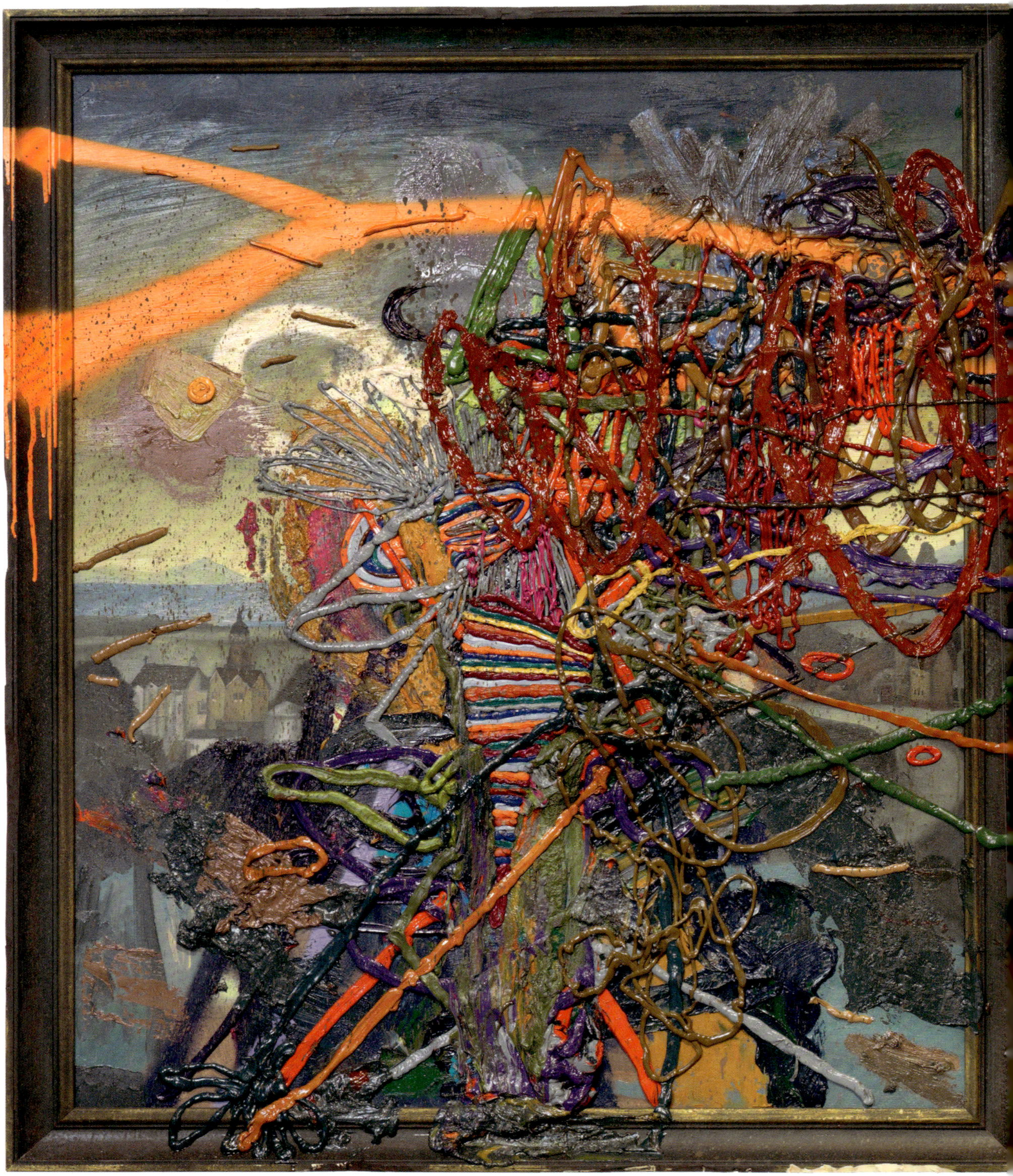

 Like a Star, Hope Fell from the Heavens Below, 2014

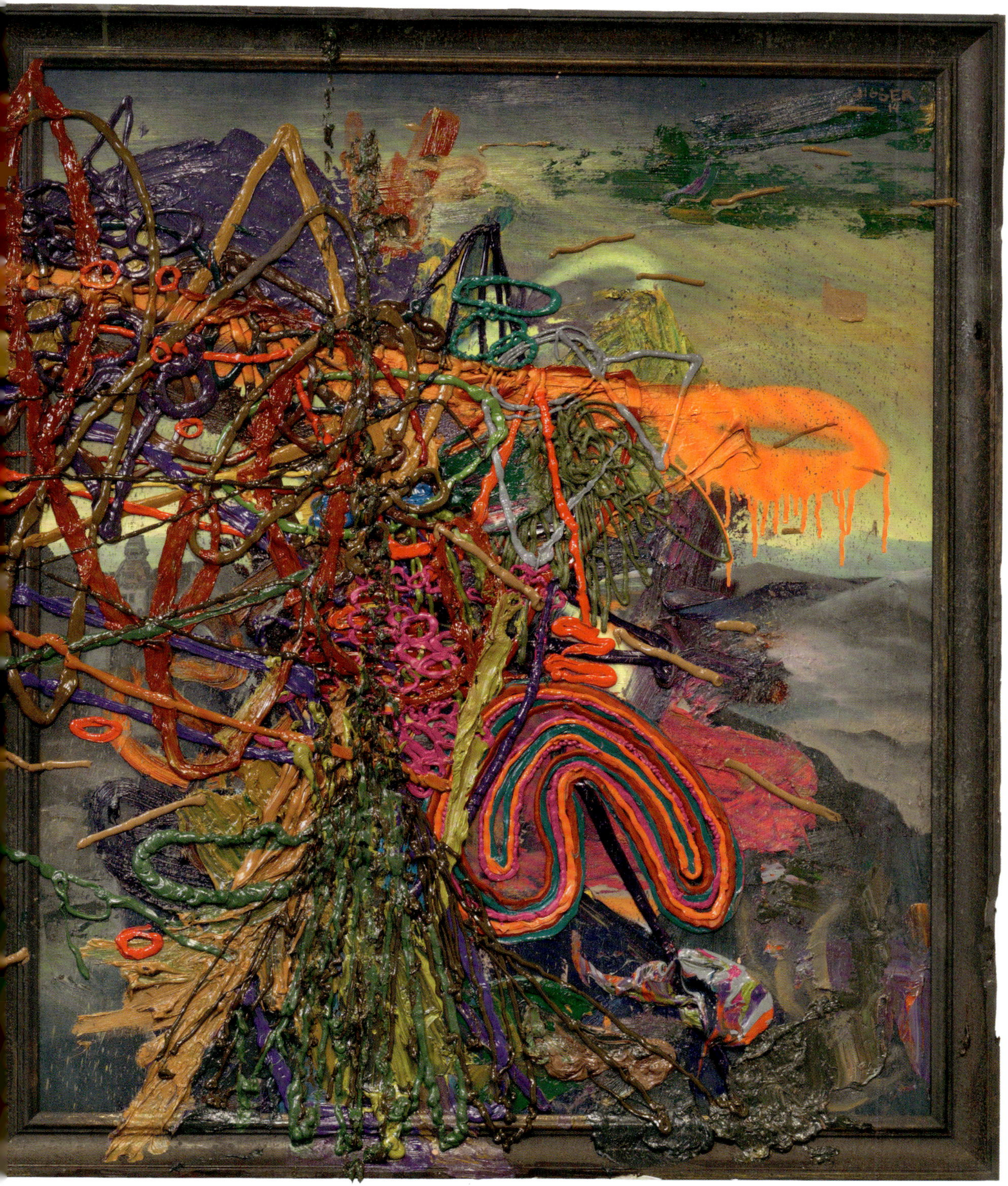

 Plane of Substantial Failure, 2014

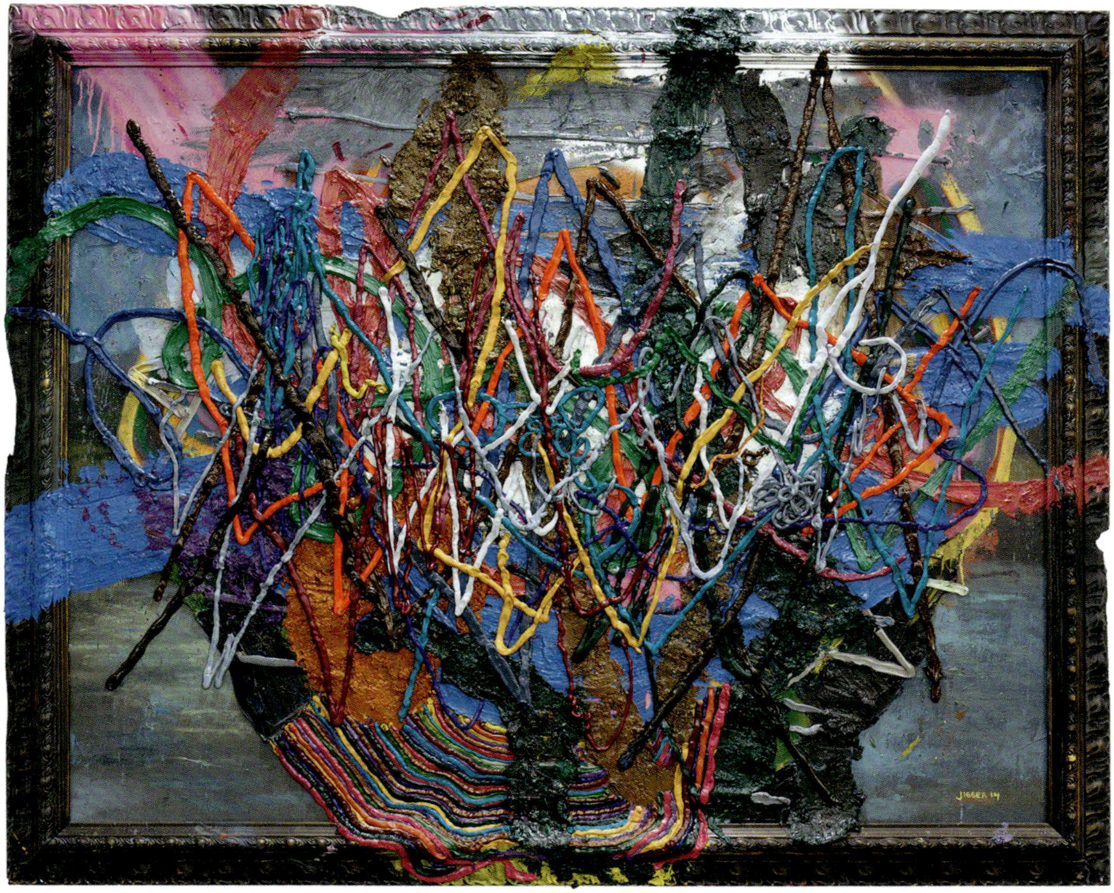

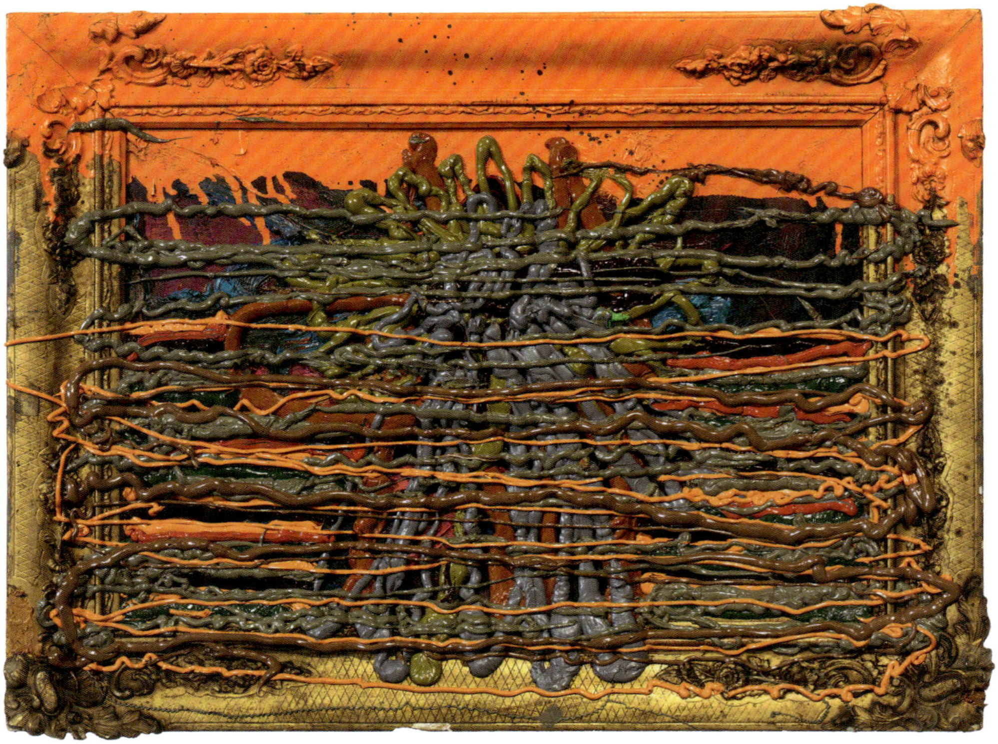

 Landscape in the Outer Kingdom of Humanities, 2014

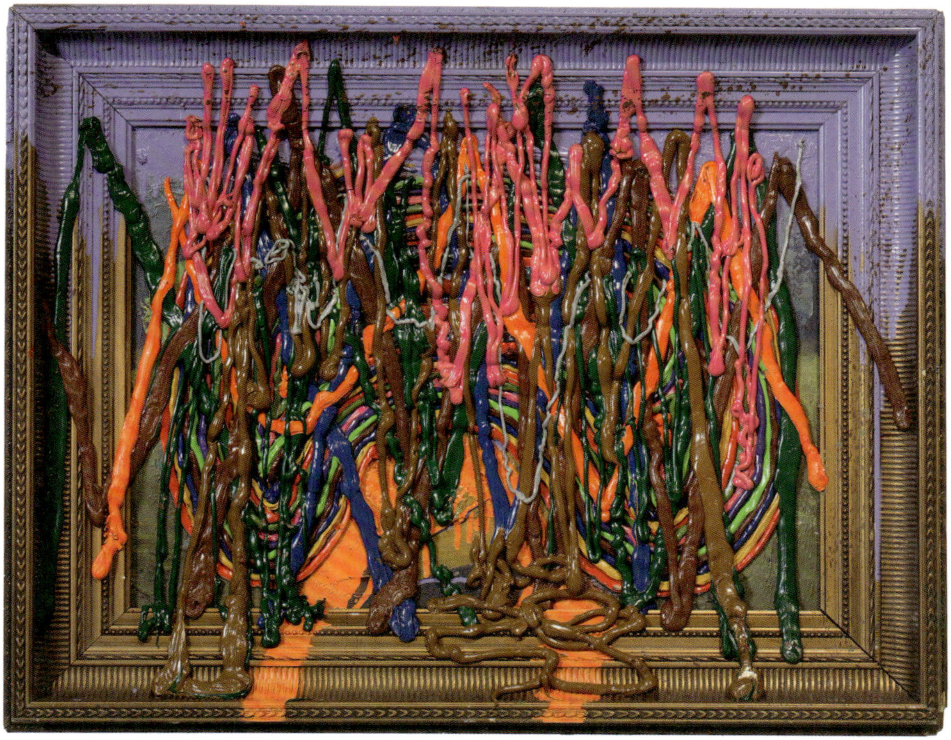

Collapsing Constellations, 2014

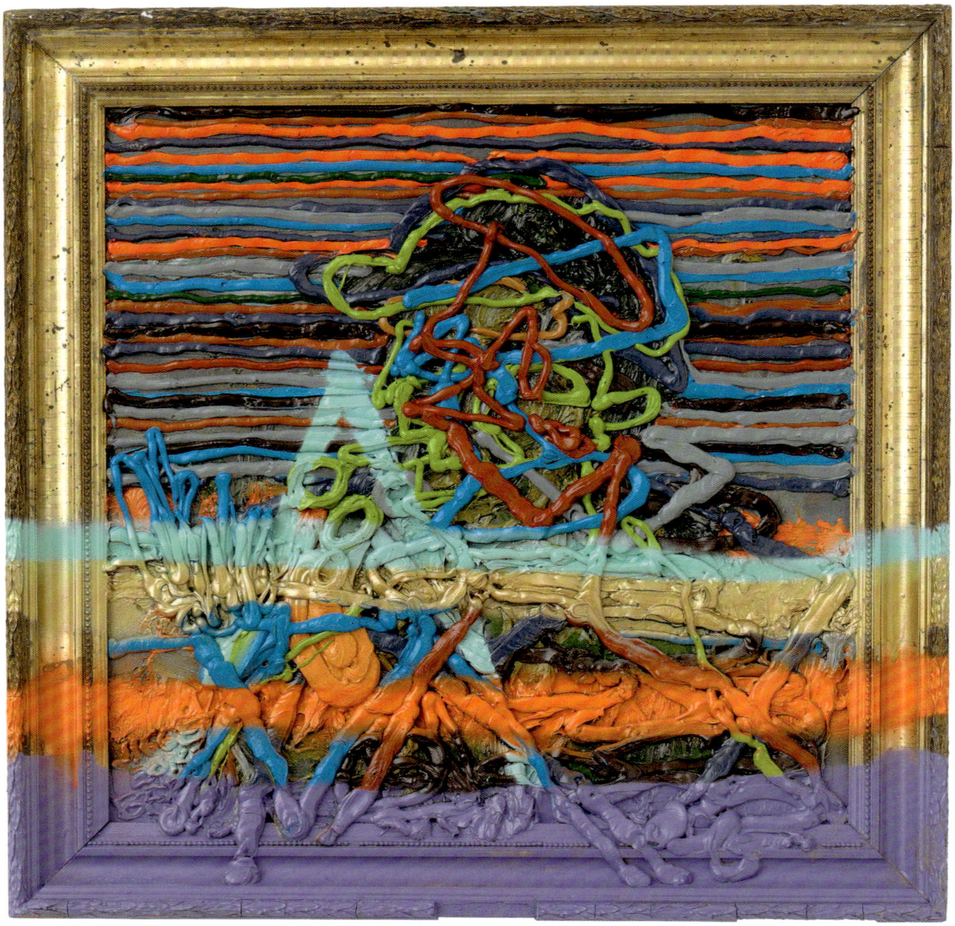

 Censored Shadow, 2014

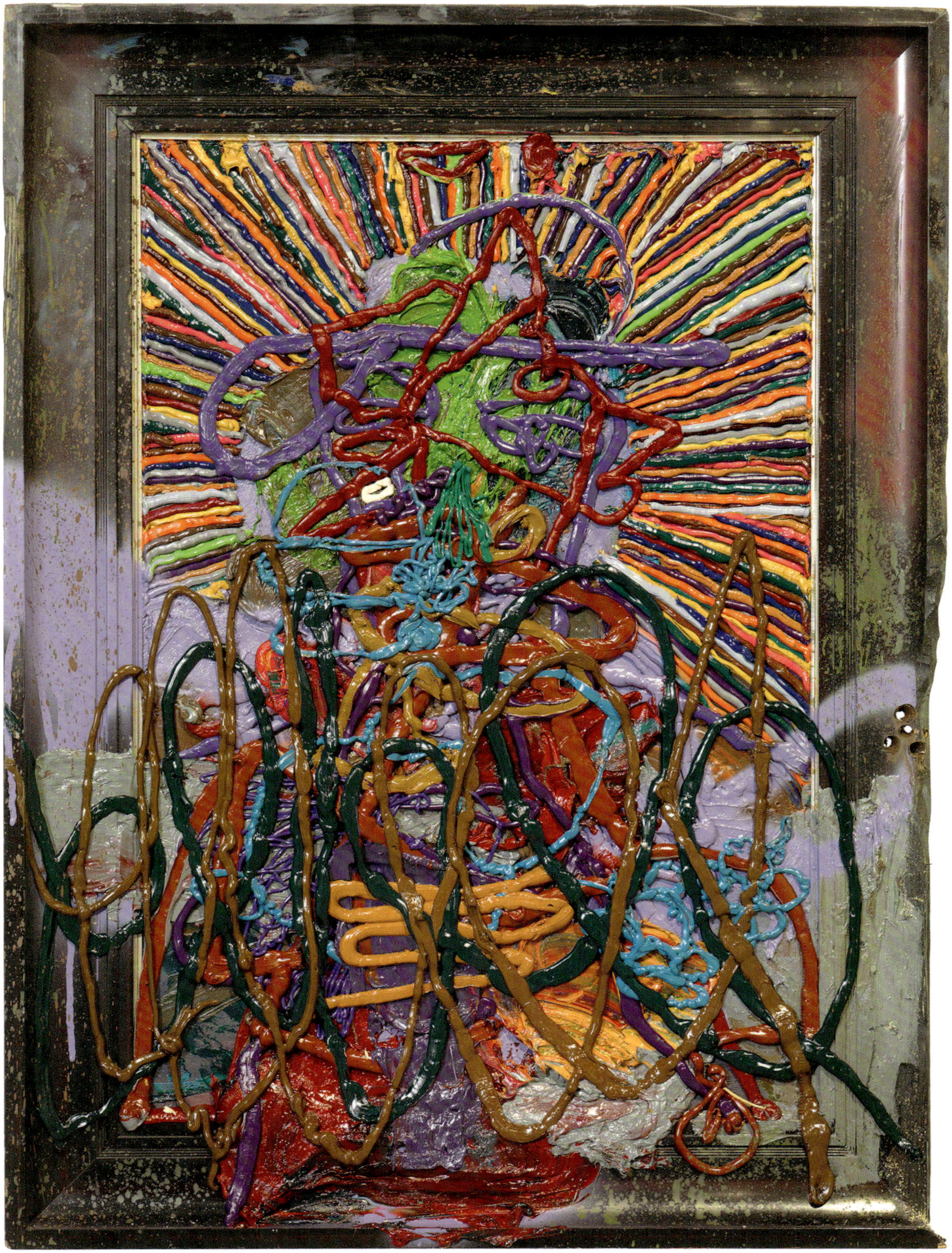

Western Style, the Painter's Eye, ir. Fine Frenzy Rolling, 2014

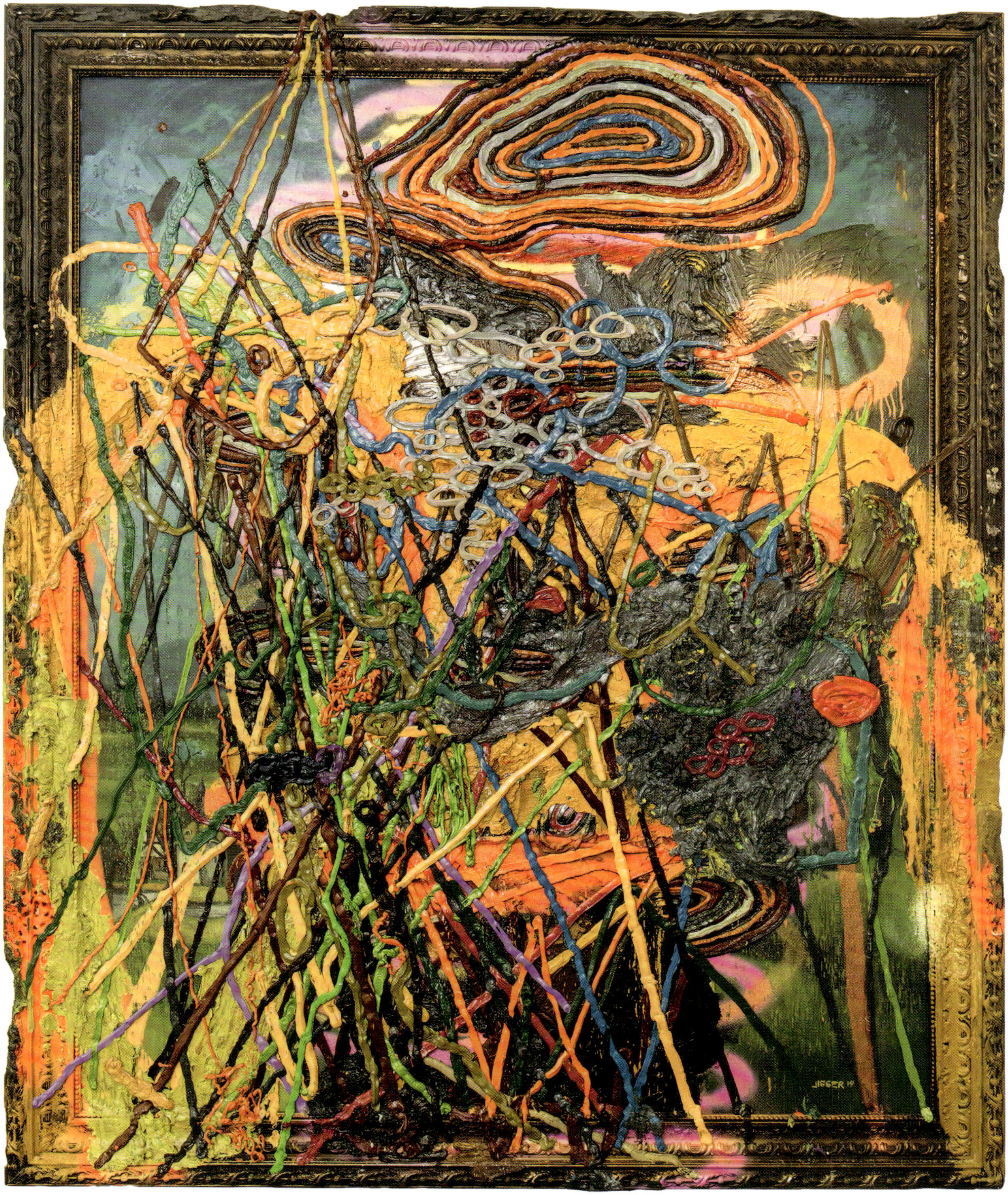

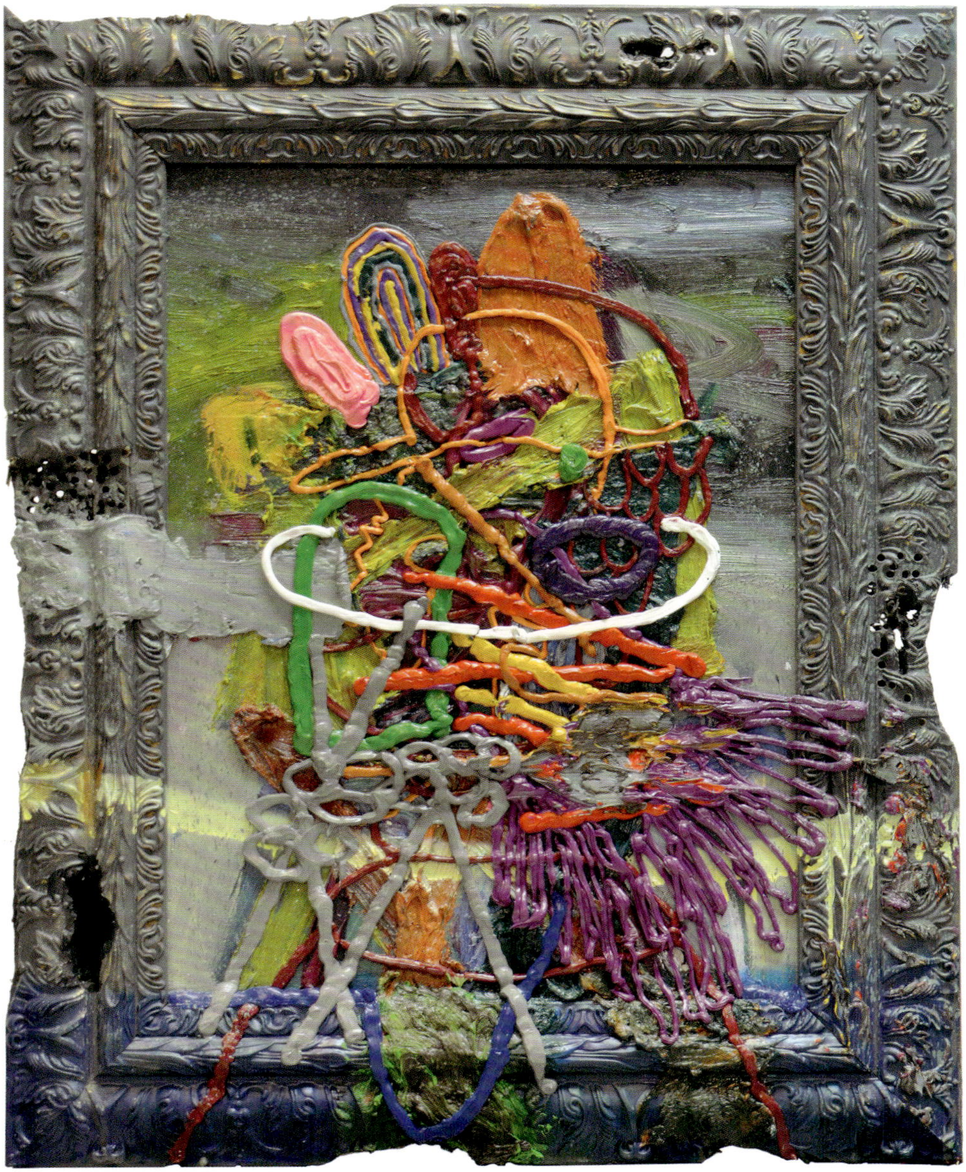

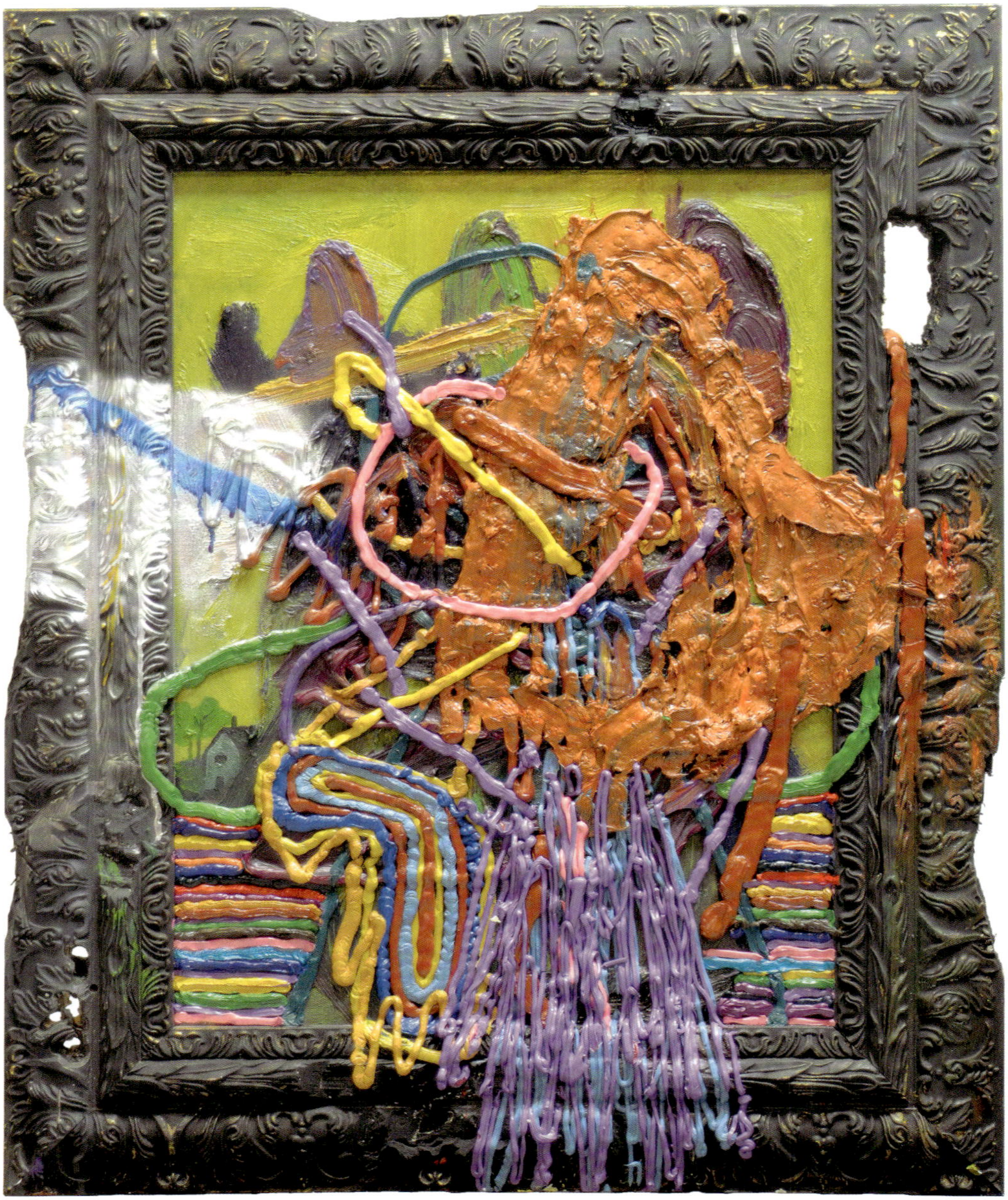

 This is an Apple, 2015

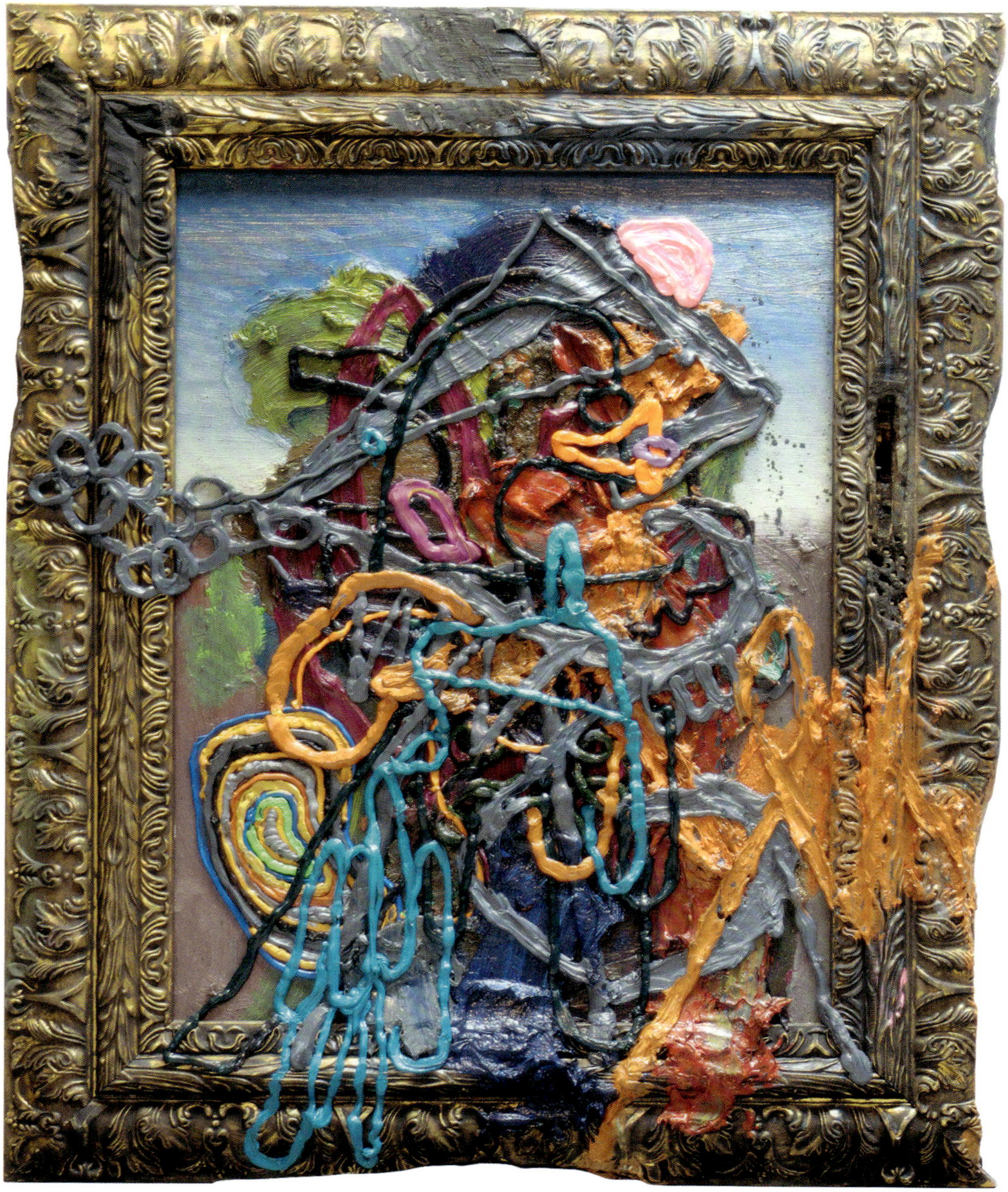

Off-beat, 2015

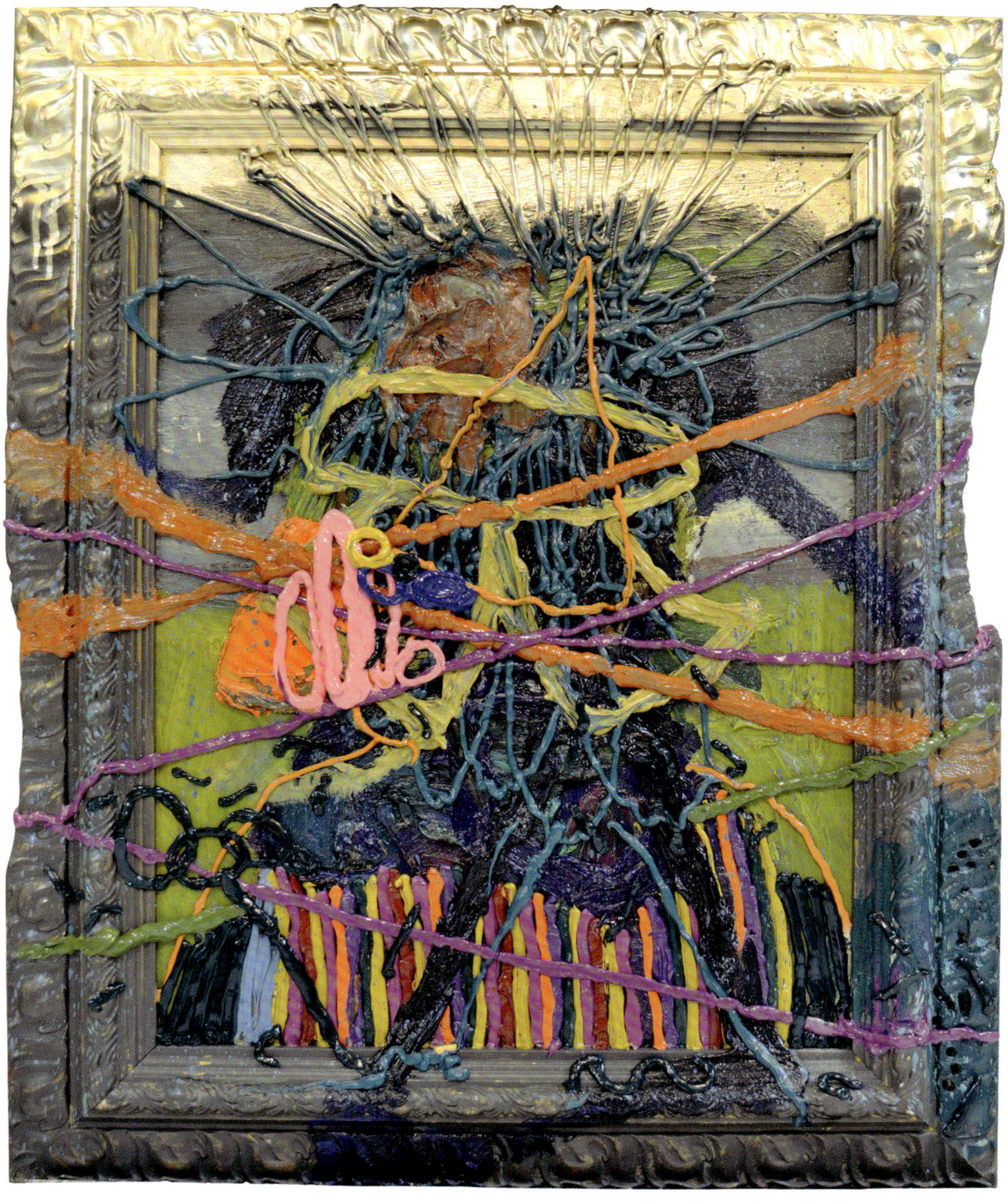

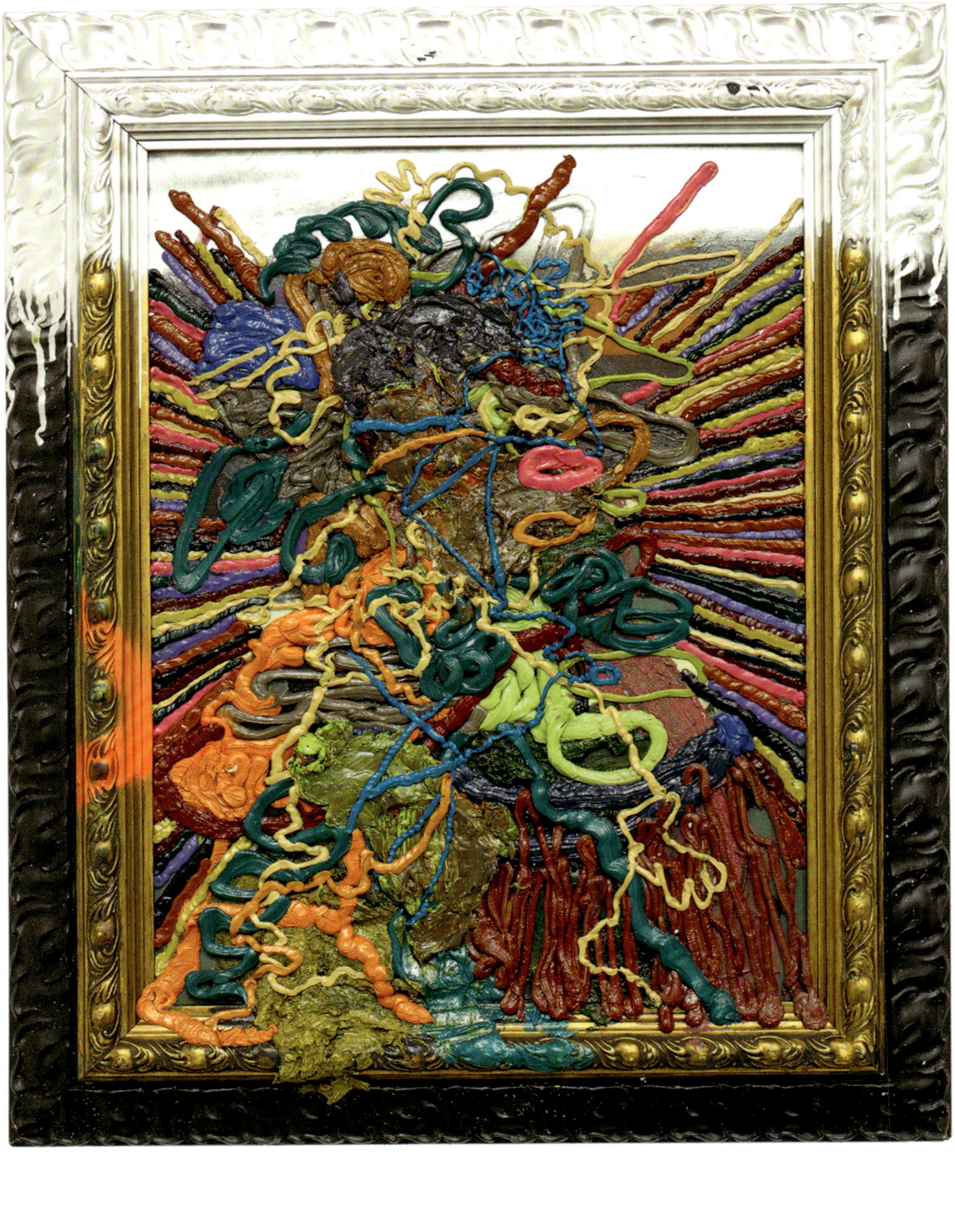

 The Fall of Chromatic Sunrise, 2014

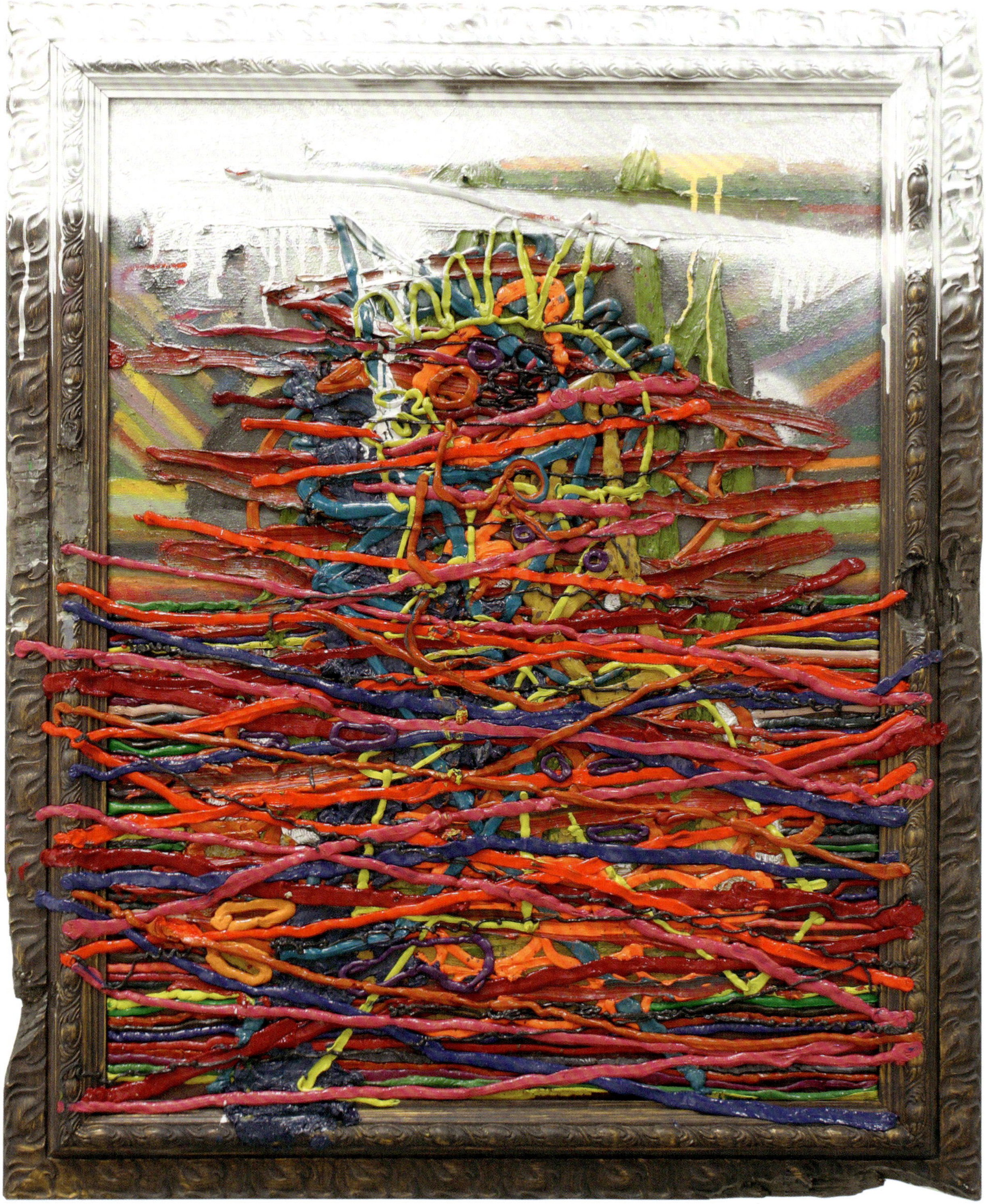

The Black and White of Yellow and Blues, 2015

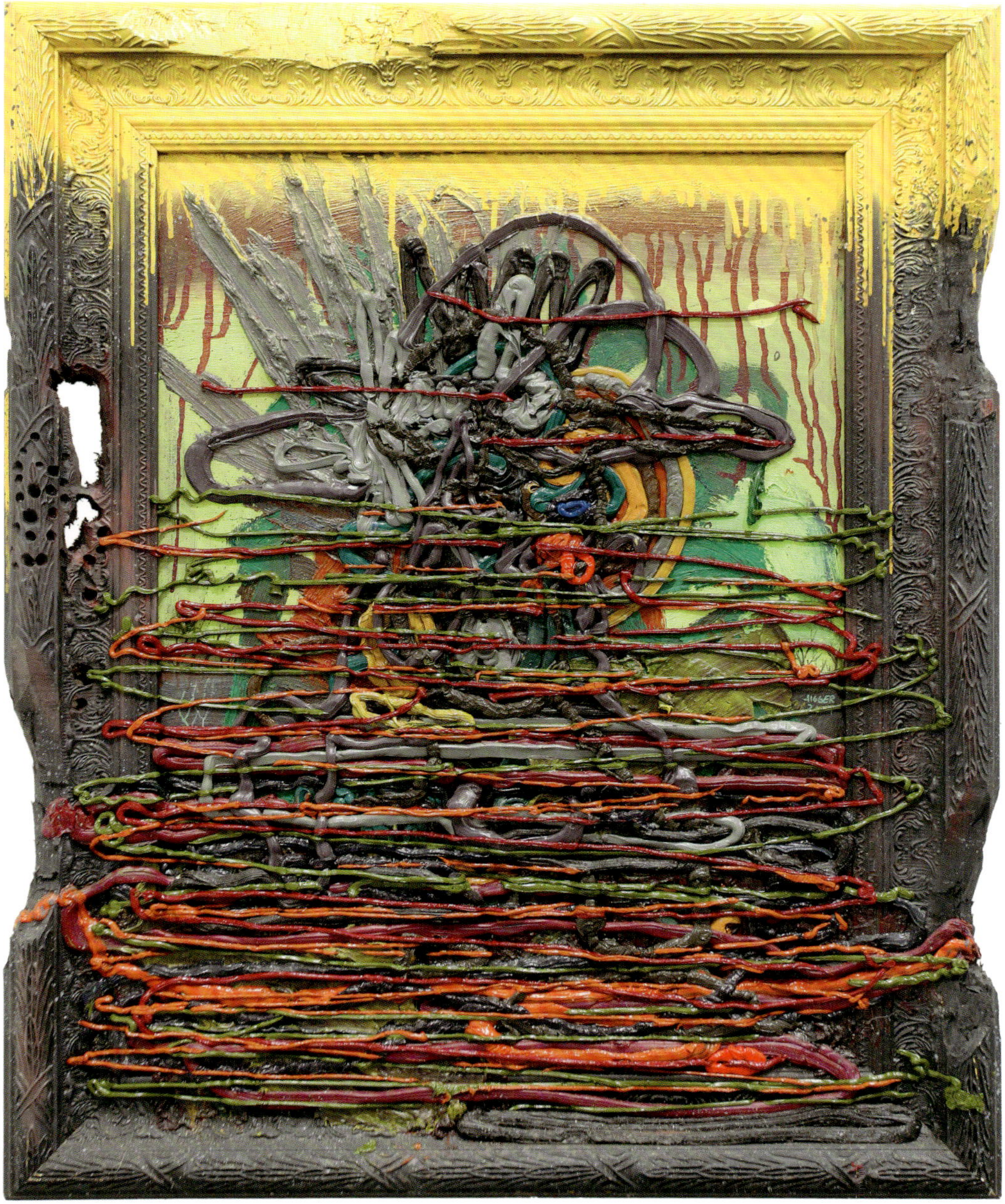

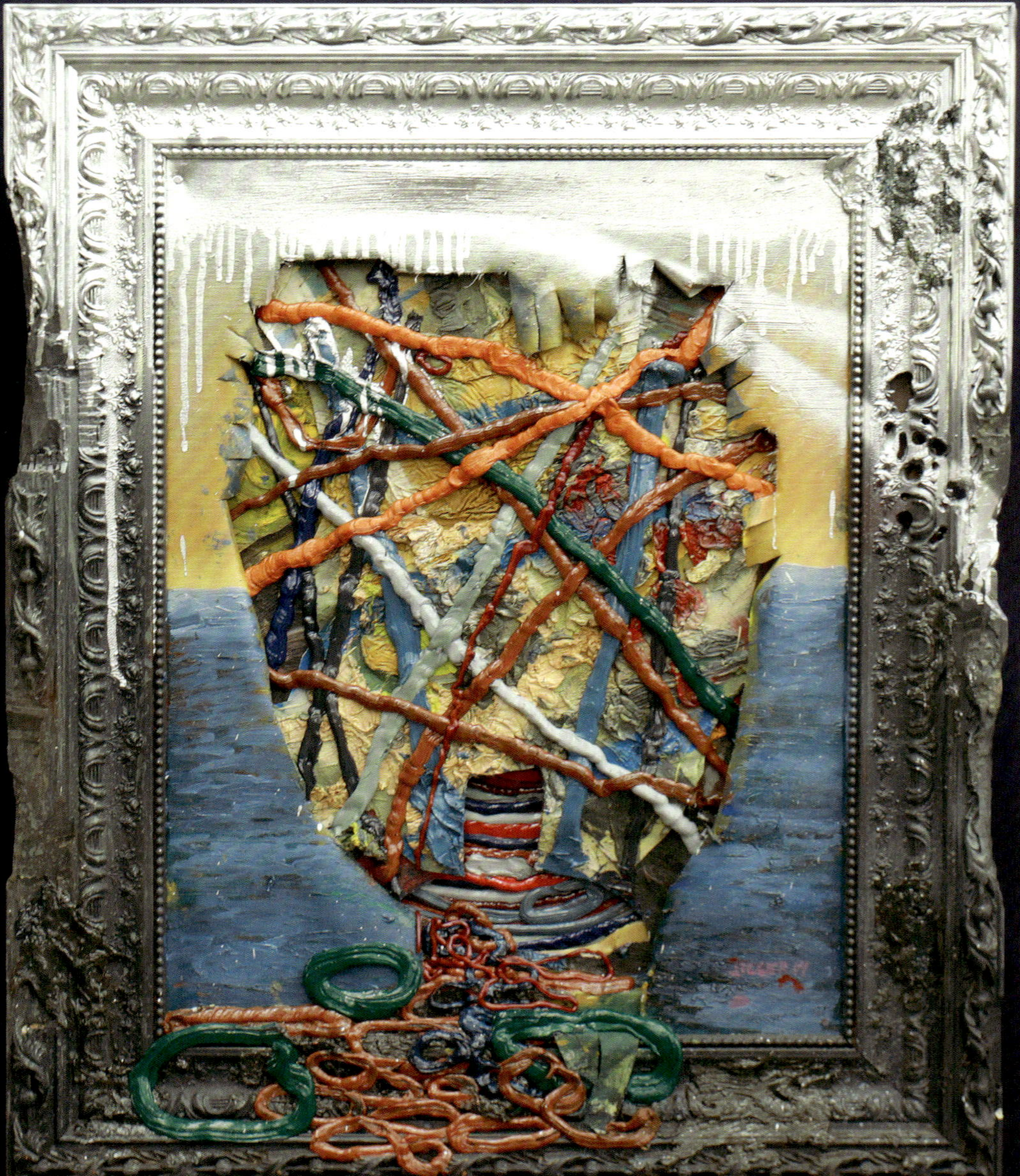

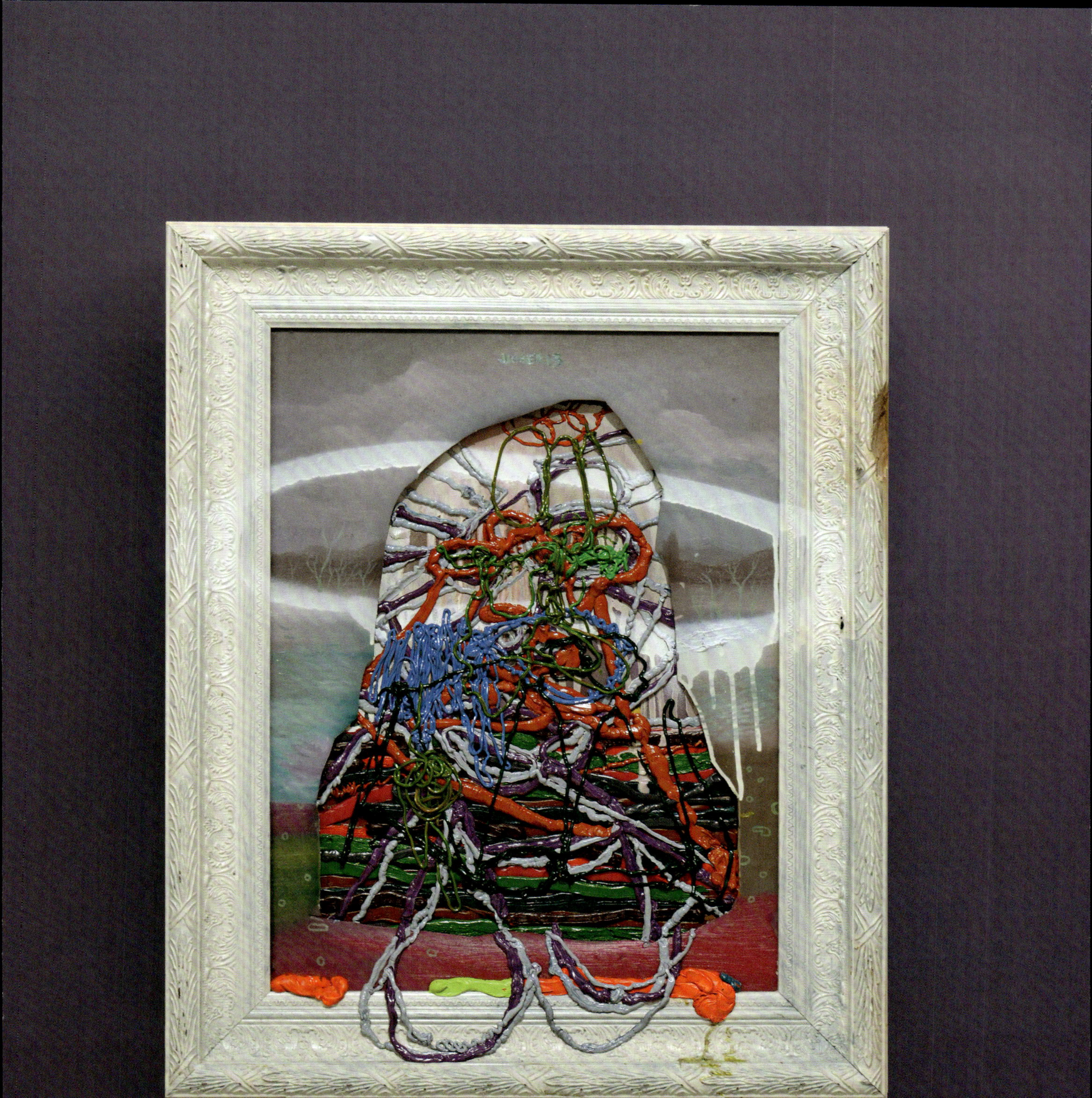

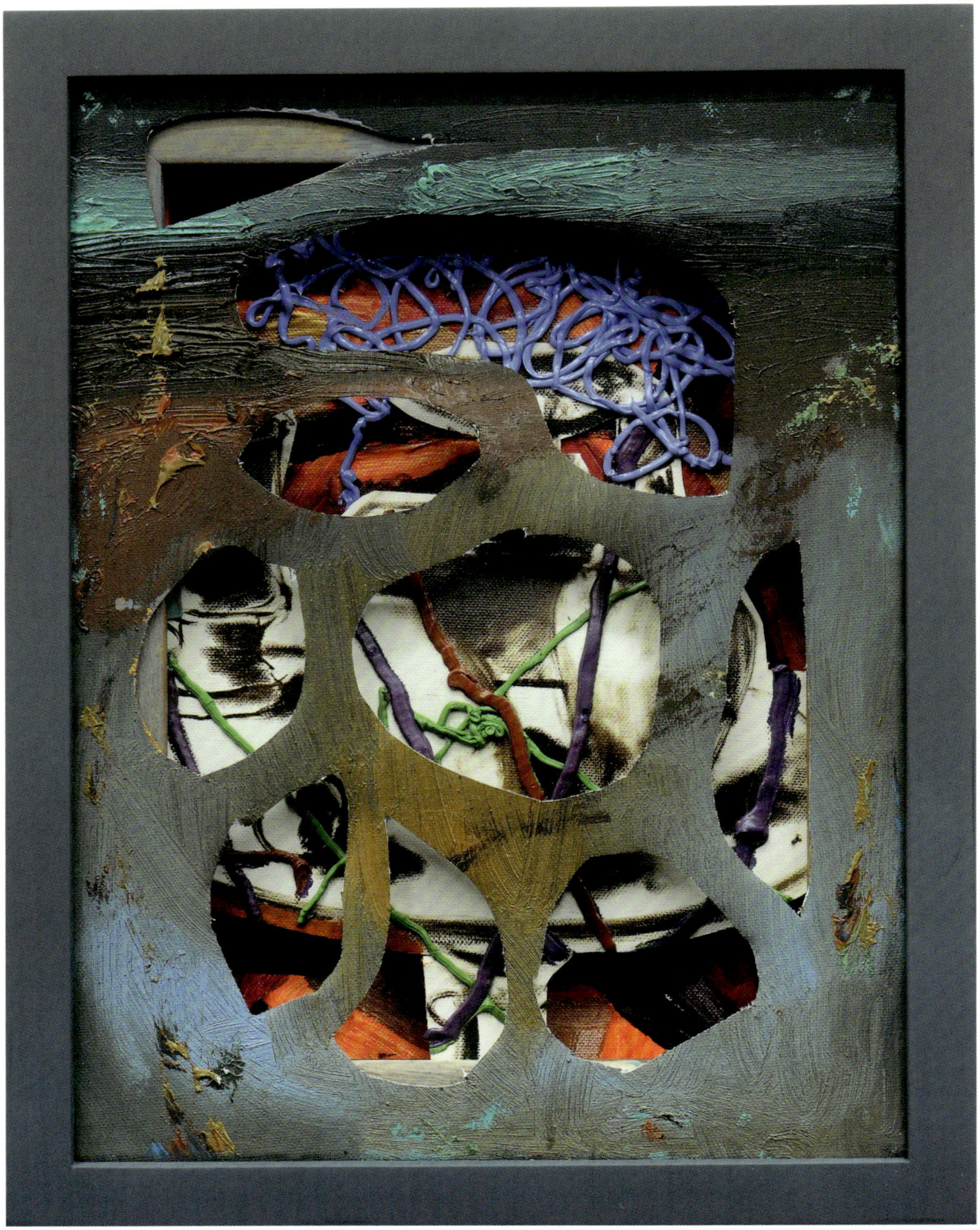

 Depth Against the Little Halos, 2013

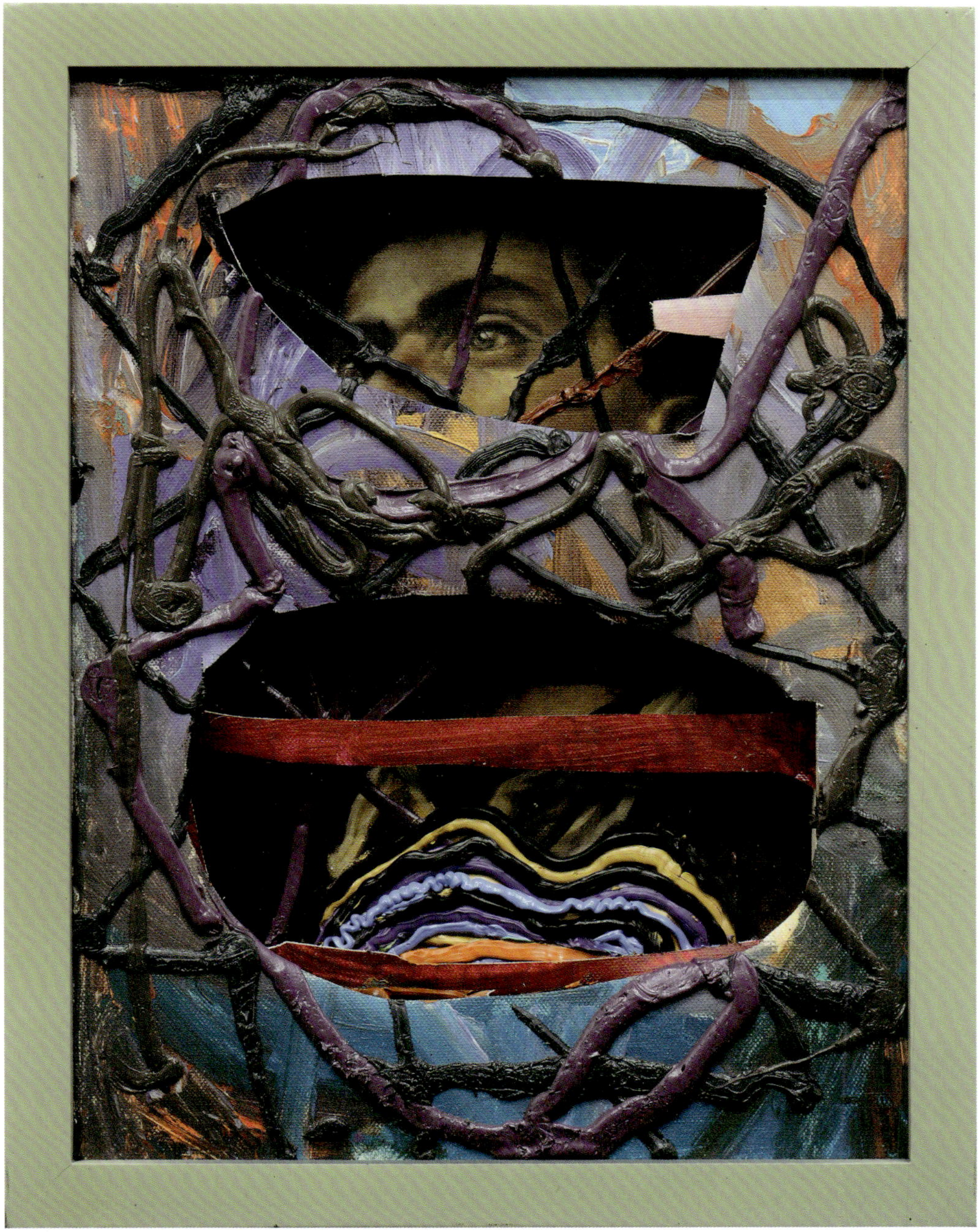

The Plastic Mathematics, 2013

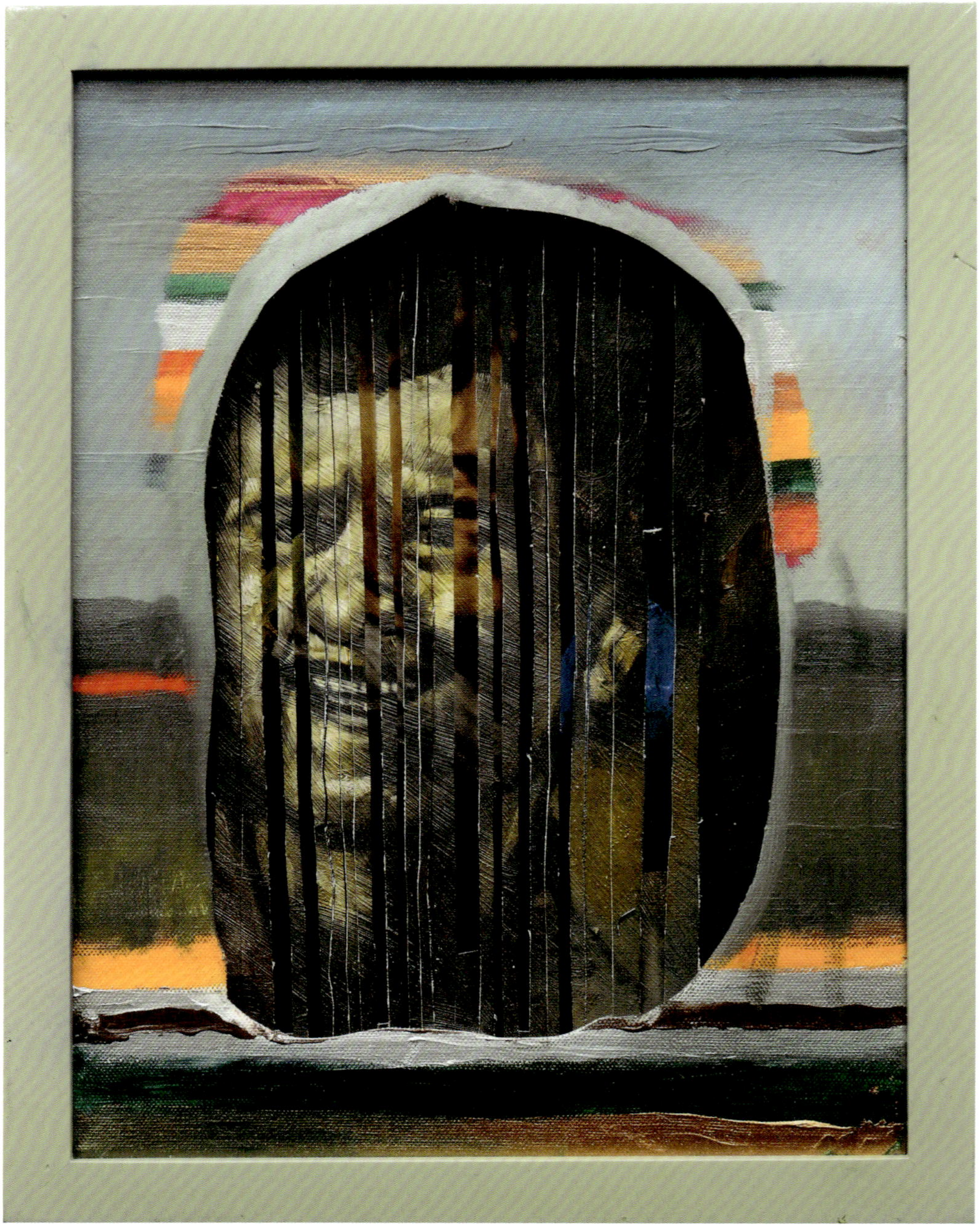

 I Can't Hear the Cracklings, 2013

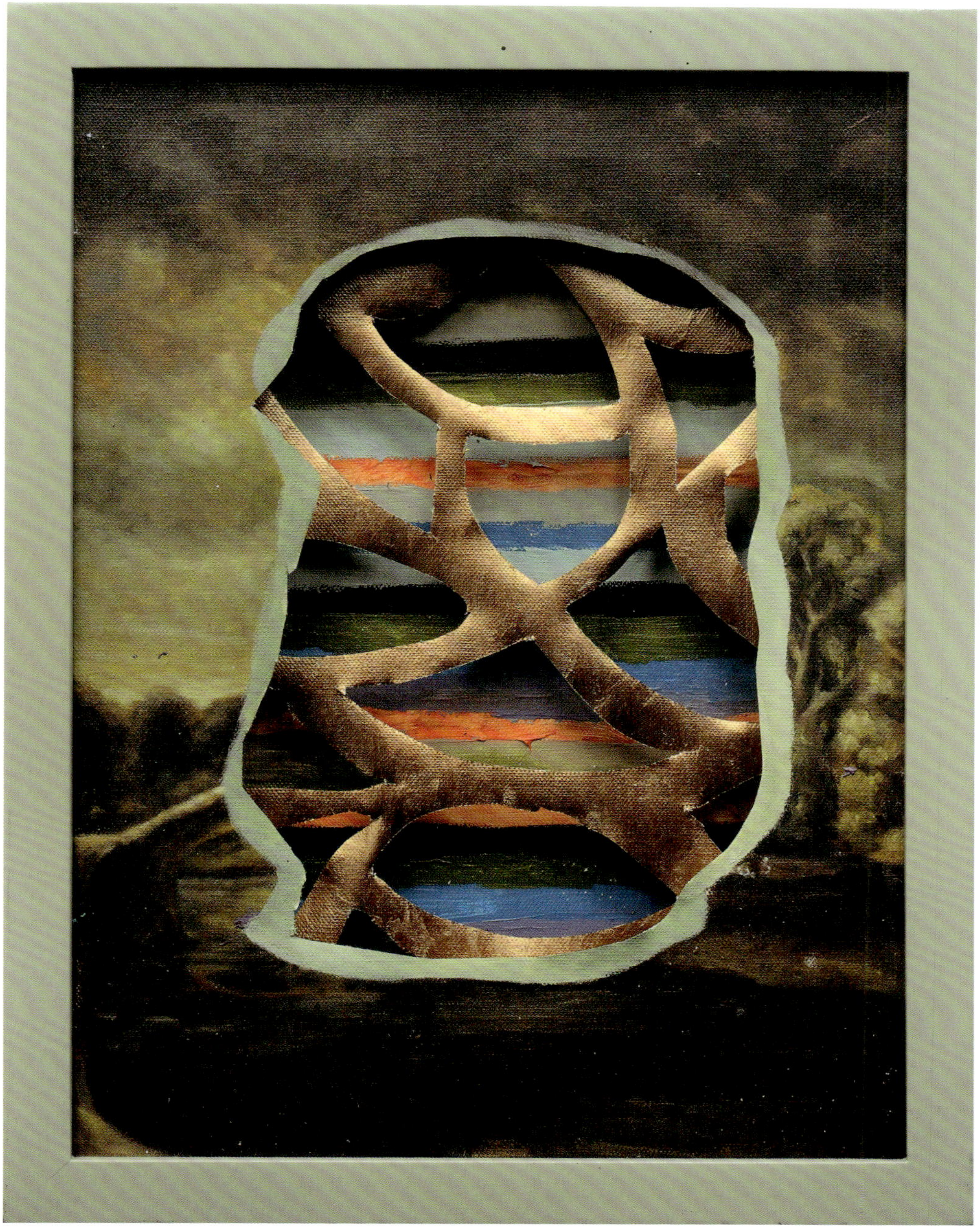

Sempiternal Landscape, 2013

 Depth from the Fall of Existence, 2013

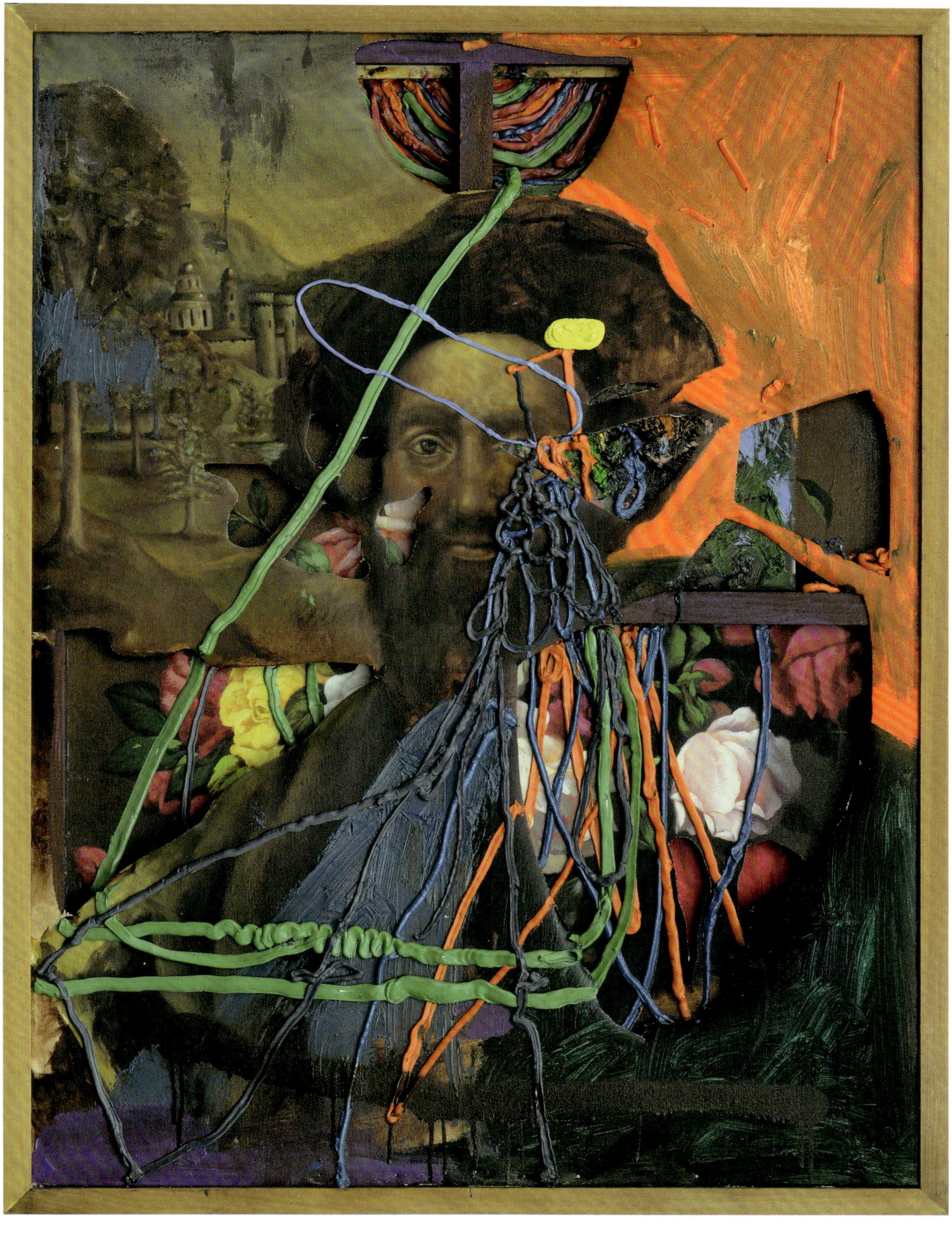

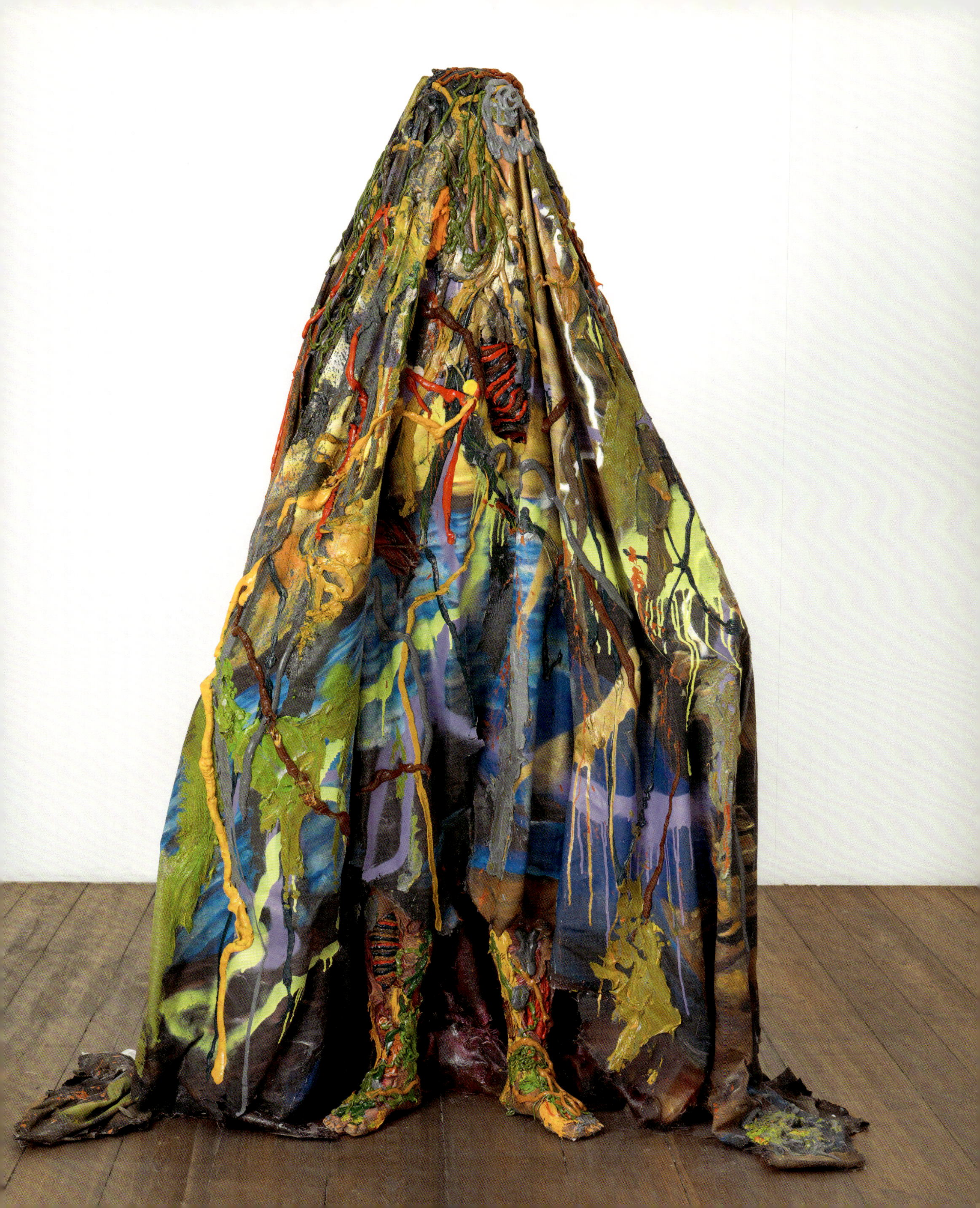

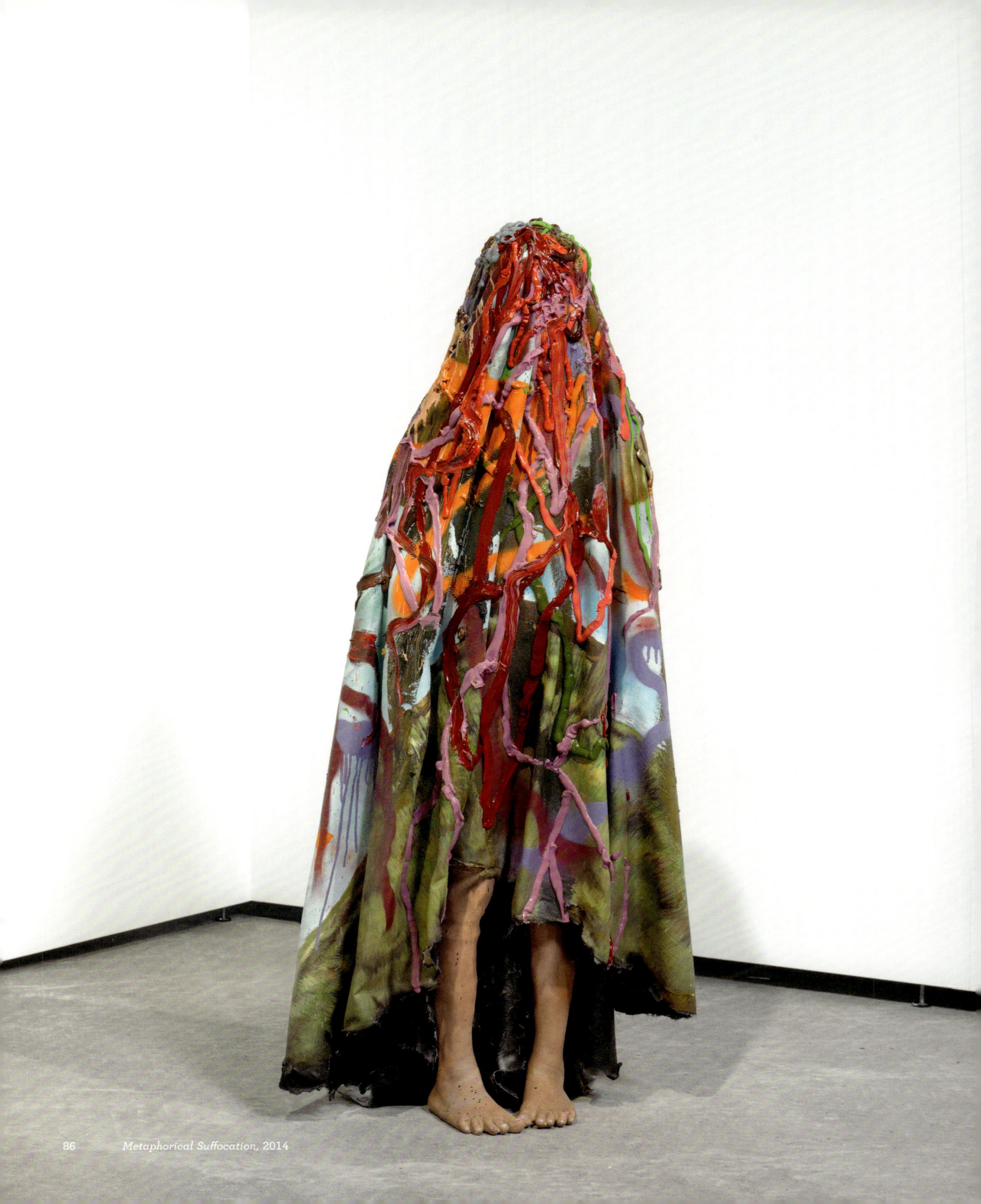

Metaphorical Suffocation, 2014

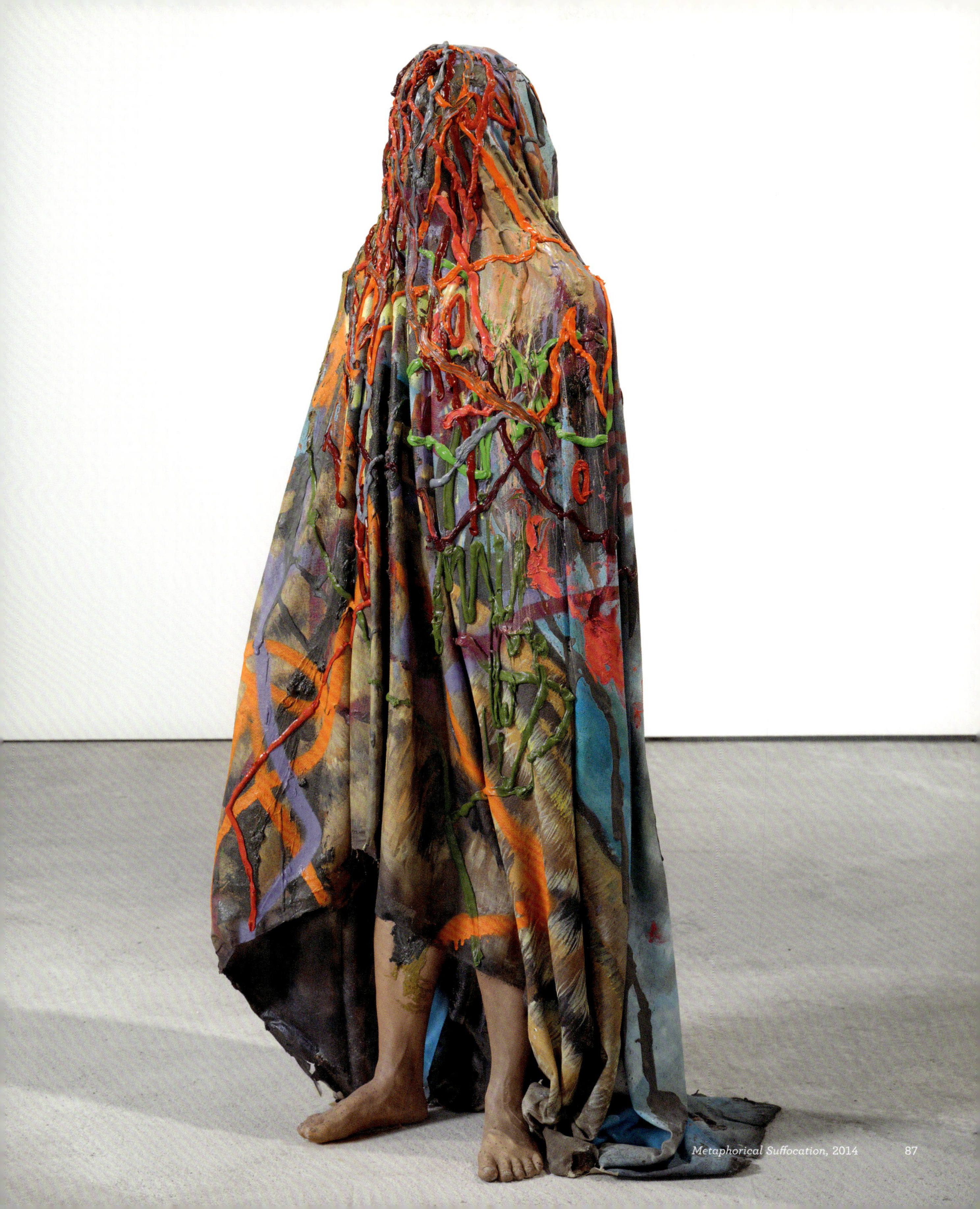

Metaphorical Suffocation, 2014

A Mark from the Periphery

Benny Nemerofsky Ramsay

There is something fascinating about the acts of painting that do not make their way into the boundaries of a finished canvas: the seemingly random smatterings of paint splashed pell-mell across studio walls and floors, the meticulous or chaotic arrangement of colors on the painter's palette. These peripheral traces of the artist's process reveal a different quality of painting: they are looser, accidental, less self-conscious. They speak a different language, one not designed for the spectator's critical gaze.

Artists have long sought to transfer the unique qualities of palettes and studio walls onto canvas, reframing these traces and accidents as the artwork itself. The results vary, although often the effect ends up feeling rather decorative, forced, or otherwise unconvincing. It is as though the defining character of this kind of mark making, its psychology and *raison d'être*, cannot cross the boundary onto the canvas: that its essence resists this intentional shift in context. It seems that the world outside the painting must remain marginal in order to speak—that it cannot convincingly appear as *inside*. It cannot be given such distinct, focused subjectivity.

Artist Jigger Cruz succeeds in transplanting the elusive characteristics of this peripheral painting onto the canvas by affording it instead a shared subjectivity, involving it as but one character in a larger struggle between the *inside* and *outside* of the picture. In fact, he does not separate the two realms: he juxtaposes them one atop the other. In this way, the experience of looking at Cruz's oeuvre is more like seeing the finished painting, the palette, and the paint-encrusted studio walls all at once, collapsed into a single visual field.

Gazing upon a work by Cruz, one immediately comprehends that there are two paintings at work—or rather, two separate acts of painting. There is a thick, three-dimensional layer of brightly colored paint, sometimes squeezed directly from the tube in criss-crossing stripes or a kind of stream-of-consciousness pattern. This layer—dominant, taking up space, commanding attention—acts as a mask over another painting, one that is almost obliterated yet still familiar and easy to read. It is frequently a portrait or a landscape, painted in a classical Western style, acquired or perhaps copied by Cruz. Even though buried under a heavy lattice of multicolored paint, the basic compositional elements of the classical painting can be traced and understood by the viewer, if not with their eyes, then with their mind.

This mental reassembly of the painting underneath, this "re-membering," is a testament to the degree in which traditions of Western painting are etched into the consciousness of each individual in our current historical moment. One need not be born into a European or American cultural setting to be amply exposed to the contours and obsessions of Western aesthetic discourse. This series of pictorial rules and tendencies have proliferated to such a degree that they are widely understood as a kind of visual truth that shapes the way people across the globe experience the visible world.

Faced with the layers of paint and meaning that tremor and undulate in Cruz's works, the spectator is invited to question which parts of the painting are *above*, and which are *below*. The eye oscillates back and forth between the visible fragments of the classical painting and the mountainous terrain of Cruz's streaks of paint. These are shifts in color and texture, two- and three-dimensionality, but also a series of compositional shifts, as

Cruz's intervention disrupts the painting's fundamental anatomy, cancelling out horizon lines and defying depth of field.

But the power of the classical painting is not so easily blotted out. It may lie physically below Cruz's dramatic, defiant intervention, but its psychic authority cannot be eclipsed. It remains so significant, so legible, that its presence is arguably the defining feature of the final artwork. The classical painting shines through, gazing back indifferently, assuming dominion not only over Cruz's mark making but also the viewer who gazes upon it. So while the eye's movement seeks to synthesise the two visual fields, the different paintings never truly coalesce into one.

In this way Cruz's approach to painting speaks to us of the burden of history. Not only the burden all artistic acts are subjected to, but also the specific burden borne by non-Western artists whose artistic production, place in society, and imaginative processes are inescapably mediated by the Western art historical narrative. Cruz's paintings reveal the inevitability of the matter, the extent to which Western cultural imperialism cannot be escaped. Indeed, the artist brings us to the realisation that even the mere act of squeezing oil paint from a tube is an entry into discourse. His paintings can be seen as attempts to cope with this legacy, a kind of interaction and engagement that resists easy classification. Cruz wrestles with the weight of art history, and it is this struggle—rather than the hope for a victorious outcome—that is key to his artistic activity.

The struggle is beautiful and passionate. As Cruz paints over existing surfaces charged with meaning, he leaves room for interpretation, for doubt, for the very equivocacy of the paint that lies splattered on a studio floor. There is a captivating ambiguity as to whether his interventions bring us closer to the truth of the painting upon which he is acting, or if they take us even further away, creating an impenetrable barrier not only to the initial composition, but to the emotional potential it holds. One cannot say for certain if Cruz's intervention is about destruction or reverence, aggression or ennui. The artist seems alternately furious with, and bored by, the cultural baggage with which he is forced to contend.

The struggle is not simply conceptual, but also deeply physical. Part of what is so captivating about Cruz's painting interventions is their decidedly performative style. The viewer encounters energetic evidence of the act of painting: loud, visible traces of the painter's gestures that are ostensibly absent from the so-called masterful application of paint that lies beneath. This second application acts as an aggressive reminder that every act of painting is also an act of the body.

The marks are made not only with pigment and tubes of oil paint, but also scissor gouges in the canvas, sawed-out corners of the frame, and sometimes streaks of bright spray paint. These tools and devices bring with them their own set of associations, positioning Cruz's interventions within the language of graffiti, and discourses of vandalism in particular. Vandalism enters the frame with cultural and historical weight, posing questions about the fixity of an image's physical properties and semiotic power.

For the destruction of property that is implied by vandalism reveals an expectation of permanence, of finalness to the object being vandalised, as though this object were, in fact, somehow complete, perfect in its pre-vandalised form. It is this aura of permanence that gives the classical painting its authority, its arrogance, and it is this aspect that Cruz resists.

Cruz's actions challenge the viewer to consider the life of a painting, both materially and immaterially, more complexly: to unpack the neutrality of the painted image. For long before it reached Cruz's hands, the painting he copies was subjected to a series of acts, both physical and semiotic, that essentially added layers of meaning and significance as influential as Cruz's acts of so-called vandalism. The painting was framed, thus altering its dimensions, aesthetic properties, and monetary value. It was exhibited, spoken about, placed in a historical context, sold for a price based on prevailing art-market discourses of the time. It joined a collection in a home or perhaps a museum. It was photographed, reproduced in a catalogue or as a postcard, maybe even printed onto a silk scarf or umbrella. It was sold again. It was copied. It increased or decreased in value. Not to mention the initial act of representing a landscape or individual in the first place, interpolating the subject in a series of aesthetic and cultural discourses. In fact, where and when does the vandalism really begin?

Cruz's gouging and overpainting are perhaps more decipherable as acts of vandalism, but it is difficult to judge their position in the hierarchy of alterations and displacements of the original paintings' form and meaning that have taken place.

Cruz's mark making is therefore not random and gratuitous, but rather a challenge to the painting's neutrality, a questioning of its assumed innocence. The painting is a text; it speaks, and its message can be interpreted, among other things, as the reification of a series of cultural and political truths. Its very existence is a proclamation, and thus a provocation: one that Cruz has decided to confront face-to-face. Cruz's mark making speaks, too, but not as a lone voice. Rather, it speaks over and against the discourse that is responsible for its marginalisation. His peripheral painting moves from outside the frame onto the canvas in order to interrupt and transform dominant art-historical discourse.

As with most voices from the margins, the extent to which Cruz's mark making is heard is fragile, and only partially in its own hands. As spectators we are granted the roles of witness to, and judge of, this confrontation. The remains of Jigger Cruz's struggle offer themselves as tools with which to ask our own questions about the aesthetic forces that influence the lens through which we all filter the visual world.

Benny Nemerofsky Ramsay, born in 1973 in Montréal, is an artist and diarist. His work in sound, video, and text has been exhibited internationally, including recent exhibitions at the Frankfurter Kunstverein, Frankfurt am Main, the Kunsthistorisches Museum Wien, Vienna, and the National Gallery of Canada, Ottawa. His writing on art, memory, and the human voice has appeared in diverse art magazines including *C Magazine* and *Kapsula*, both based in Toronto, and in books on the work of artists Gunilla Josephson, Conny Karlsson Lundgren, and Shaan Syed. He lives and works in Berlin.

Caught in the Interregnum

Lisa Ito

There is a method to the proverbial madness behind the works of Jigger Cruz: a sense of continuum guiding his process of defacing and repainting art objects to produce new strategies of representation.

Part of a generation of young Filipino artists exposed to an increasingly globalized market over the past five years, Cruz has been exploring the possibilities of painting as a reflexive and transnational marker of contemporaneity.

Cruz's own story as a young Filipino painter is still an unfolding one. He studied Fine Arts at the Far Eastern University in Manila until 2007 and mounted his first solo exhibition the year after, in 2008. In 2012, he presented his first solo exhibition abroad. In this relatively short span of time, the artist has gradually steered his art practise and philosophy towards reflecting on how the cultural industry—both at the local and global levels—has, in his own words, "developed an insatiable illusionism," and also exploring the nature of painting as part of the material language of art.

The selection of works from 2012 to 2015 in this book highlights this particular phase of Cruz's practise. The artist embarks on a sweep of iconoclasm against classical painting and sculpture in the way he obscures objects beneath fresh and thick layers of pigment. In recent years, he has produced objects—ranging from paintings and sculptures to installations—and has collectively positioned them as discrete and decaying icons of academism and tradition. Contained within ornate frames or set up on pedestals, all the works are drawn over and defaced: most traces of carefully applied paint and modeling are obscured by raw, textured brushstrokes.

Distilling and Defacing Histories

The artist describes his works as highly entropic acts of personal spontaneity, and explores different approaches to painting at this stage in his personal practise. Cruz excises and exorcises all earlier traces of representation and subject matter, using vivid colors applied straight from the tube. Paint brushes are wielded like crayons or pens, cutting patterns across previously "sacred" surfaces with an intense, almost primal, vitality. Viscous pigment is squeezed and smeared, directed and deliberately drawn across canvas and frame, form and surface.

Despite the seeming dominance of anarchy and chaos across their surfaces, Cruz's works may be also, conversely, read as a conscious strategy to visualize the transitional nature of contemporary art. A strong sense of containment prevails: the will to play with the very physicality of painting—and to adhere to these formal parameters across a wide range of objects—makes his process a highly intentional and deliberate one.

Cruz applies this same method of defacement, uniformly and deliberately, across different objects. Thus his works can be encountered as a continuum of gestures, rather than as a collection of discrete and immobile objects. All forms are subsumed to Cruz's playful process of strategic destabilization. What would be otherwise seen as individual works of art are collectively and physically altered: all part of the sweeping, irreversible process of transformation.

Of his many works so far, the locus of Cruz's outlook towards art is perhaps best embodied and visualized in a sculptural series from 2014 entitled *Metaphorical Suffocation* (pp. 85–87), comprising of resin human figures entirely covered in painted canvases.

The figures vary. One, for instance, is on the cusp of adolescence, another in the prime of life. Covered in painted canvas, the figures stand apart, barefoot, exposed: all are obscured, anonymous sentinels facing an unseen threat. The boy seems unsure and tentative, his feet shuffling against each other, while the man assumes a more upright and resolute stance.

"This show is an iconoclastic representation of the suffocation of a certain dialogue between the past and the present," Cruz says about his 2014 Berlin exhibition of which the sculptures were part. Here, the artist reveals that the figure of the man is a representation of the transition from past to present: cognizant and certain of the narrative of modernity, the avant-garde march towards contemporary art and beyond. The boy figure, on the other hand, represents the shift from present to future, betraying a sense of anxiety about his prospects and current trajectories. Both figures remain covered in opaque sheets, blinded and trapped by the weight of history. Unable to move purposefully in any particular direction, both stand the risk of suffocation and ossification. They are veiled references, so to speak, to the sense of immobility confronted by contemporary artists.

The only way to move forward, Cruz's barefoot figures imply, is to feel one's way through space, intuitively navigating through the imposed darkness. One's exposed feet—shoeless and free—are the only guideposts towards clearing new spaces and cultural domains. Blindness, once shunned and scorned, becomes the very condition for redemption and the creation of the new: a state in which there is nothing for the eye to emulate or mimic. This is where Cruz reveals his veering away from the strategies outlined by modernism. Instead of aiming for the creation of a new, unparalleled and original sensibility, the artist responds by consciously appropriating, destroying, and defacing elements of the old tradition both as an artistic strategy and an end in itself.

Transnational and Transitional

Cruz's embracing of the postmodern ethos and his professed pursuit of iconoclasm are most clearly seen in his approach towards painting and sculpture, as demonstrated in his recent oil-on-canvas paintings and sculptural pieces produced between 2012 to 2015. This series is altered through his process of incising and excising, defacing and repainting, concealment and resurrection.

Cruz personally produces the paintings that he paints over afterwards, calling them "backgrounds" instead of finished works. This linguistic quirk is telling, revealing how the artist imagines the act of painting an object and creating a new artwork as formal, fundamental gestures united by the emergence of new experiences and ways of seeing. Portraits, landscapes, and genre scenes are all painted over, inhabited, and overwritten by the presence of pigment. Thus the creation of representation and subject matter are not the end goals of art, but merely constitute one facet of artistic production and experience.

The process of alteration is vital to the concept of painting as a physical object, removed from history and iconography. Cruz chooses random images from existing paintings, culled from what he terms as the "conventional era of the Old Masters," and treats them as physical surfaces rather than subject matter. A play between depth and surface, two- and three-dimensionality ensues as Cruz alters his backgrounds by applying paint—squeezed and drawn across, dipped and dripping, or seemingly randomly covered—across their surface images. Often, he leaves some works still wet or partially revealing the layers underneath—caught in the act of fusing old and new. Cruz also draws numerous references to the language of artistic tradition and history in his choice of titles for the individual works, seemingly culled from random snippets of art jargon and anecdotal narratives.

Cruz has also made a series of oil-on-wood sculptures and used, irregularly shaped canvases (pp. 23–33). These started appearing in earlier solo exhibitions such as *Spatial Soother* (West Gallery, Manila, 2012) and continue to be conceptually connected to his more recent works due to his fidelity towards process.

Cruz's choice of using discarded, often damaged, frames for the works is, likewise, a conscious reference to the weight of tradition and the containment posed by history. Some frames are quite ornate and embellished, others are minimalist and functional. But both styles of containment span the range of traditions that Cruz's sense of iconoclasm responds to: the conservatism of the academic and classical traditions of Western European art as well as the modernist bent of the turn-of-the-century avant-garde movements. Some of his sculptural works, on the other hand, are mounted on pedestals, in reference to traditional methods of displaying art objects.

Obscuring most references to figuration and subject matter, Cruz's resulting paintings and sculptures collectively emphasize the tangible, physical encounter with paint: the interplay of color and dimension, texture and surface. Extending beyond the modernist fascination with pushing and extending the limits of representation towards non-representation, Cruz appears to be reveling in the plastic properties of paint. Here, he clearly takes delight in exploring the affective physicality of colors and pigment: seen and smelled, felt and experienced. Through the rawness of gesture and texture, Cruz hopes to engage in an experiential dialogue of sorts with his viewers and to make tangible the act of communicating with the work.

Protracted Interregnum

In the history of modern art, the exploration of the physical properties of form and medium eventually led to the exploration of non-representational or abstract work. Cruz's gestural works, however, cannot be easily relegated to an extension of the type of Abstract Expressionism as practiced in post-war New York, best embodied by American artist Jackson Pollock's drip-paintings. The latter takes the capturing of pure gesture as an end goal of painting, deploying the body as a center of energy; Cruz's works, on the other hand, emphasize gestural painting as a means of concealment and ravaging, calling attention to the physical existence of paint itself, beyond the individual touches of the painter's expression.

Moreover, the images birthed by Cruz's own hand deviate vastly from the more frenetic energy given off by gestural abstraction. One may detect in the chaos of Cruz's concealments particular and recurring motifs: waves and ripples, rings and loops, organic outlines mimicking scribbles, and stripes laid precisely side by side, all casually yet clearly traversing the surface. One does not end up producing these forms without some degree of control steering the painter's hand. These patterns and forms, in this light, are not entirely products of spontaneous automatism in their intent to cover, overlap, and conceal. Instead, they point to a deliberate, almost meditative, practise of painting: one that pursues formal purity and expression as a form of purging and catharsis.

This approach towards art-making straddles earlier practises, such as collage and action painting, and recalls the entropic energy of predominantly subaltern practises such as graffiti. Cruz employs mixed strategies to produce these works, which cannot be sufficiently apprehended through the language of formal abstraction alone, but must also be seen through the lenses of appropriation and pastiche.

How does this place Filipino culture and tradition within a wider contemporary framework? The art historical interfaces from which Cruz's art also stems must be taken into consideration too. Filipino art, for instance, maintains a strong tradition of Realism—from turn-of-the-century academic painting during the period of Hispanic colonization to postwar, post-independence movements such as Neo-Realism and Social Realism. Yet it also harbors a sustained exploration of non-representational art and abstraction, influenced by the tradition of postwar abstraction in the United States. Still, meeting points between the two trajectories of representational and non-representational art have been few and far between. In this light, Cruz's work as an artist can be seen as an attempt to connect or draw some points across these discursive and visual gaps, probing possible interfaces between the two.

What are the symbolic implications of Cruz's foray into such hybrid territory, across time and space? For one, his emphasis on defacement as an artistic process also connotes a parallel reclaiming and rewriting of history, identity, and the present—concepts that the practise of representation has made possible and visible in the past. Gestural abstraction is employed as a means of erasure and effacement, critique and construction. In attempting to visually and experientially reconcile the condition of contemporaneity with a distant, often conflicting, past, Cruz's works can be read as signifiers of the protracted interregnum: giving form to the complex state of flux that characterizes the production of contemporary art.

In the end, the lens of history may very well be the best means by which Cruz's work can be weighed. The artist's strategy of exposing the embedded nature of painting within canonized traditions emphasize its capacity for being wielded reflexively. In doing so, he affirms the very potency and viability of painting as a form of artistic production, all the way from the distant past and, possibly, into the future that lies ahead.

Lisa Ito, born 1980 in Manila, lives in Quezon City where she teaches art history and theory at the College of Fine Arts, University of the Philippines, Diliman. She has written essays on art for exhibitions, books, and other publications, including *Pananaw – Philippine Journal of Visual Arts*, *FOCAS: Forum on Contemporary Art and Society*, and Francis Francisco, ed., *Without Walls: A Tour of Philippine Painting at the Turn of the Millennium* (Pasig City, 2010). She is a member of the Concerned Artists of the Philippines (CAP) and the Young Critics Circle Film Desk.

List of Works

p. 5
Damn! For a Poor Flesh 1 and *2*, 2012
Oil on wood
Approx.
15 × 8 × 10 cm each
Private collection

pp. 6–7
Tracing Mental Paradise, 2014
Oil on found object
55 × 28 cm
Private collection, Singapore

p. 9
Crawling from the Wreckage, 2015
Oil and spray paint on canvas and wooden frame
163 × 132 cm

p. 11
Disruption, 2013
Oil and spray paint on canvas and wooden frame
80 × 65 cm
Private collection, Milan, Italy

pp. 12/13
Remix 1 and *2*, 2012
Oil on canvas and wooden frame
Diptych
120 × 94 cm each
Private collection, Italy

p. 14
In the Landscape of Contradictions, 2012
Oil and spray paint on canvas and wooden frame
140 × 110 cm
Private collection, Milan, Italy

p. 15
Come Like Spoiled Bells in Sudden Wind and High, 2011
Oil on canvas and wooden frame
156 × 203 cm
Private collection, Italy

p. 16
Mystification of the False Truth, 2012
Oil and spray paint on canvas and wooden frame
119 × 94 cm
Private collection

p. 17
Finitudes Against the Distortion, 2012
Oil on canvas and wooden frame
119 × 94 cm
Private collection

p. 19
A Pause in the Triumph of Existence, 2013
Oil on canvas and wooden frame
193 × 163 cm
Private collection

p. 20
Blares of the Opposite, 2013
Oil and spray paint on canvas and wooden frame
163 × 193 cm
Private collection

p. 21
Platforms of Dispositional Overtone, 2014
Oil and spray paint on canvas and wooden frame
157 × 178 cm
Private collection, Philippines

pp. 22/23
Between Planes and Parallels, 2014
Oil and spray paint on canvas and wooden frame
Triptych
61 × 154 cm
SEACO Collection

p. 25
Embrace of the Duchampian Impulse 3, 2012
Oil on canvas and wooden frame
43 × 63 cm
Private collection

p. 26
Embrace of the Duchampian Impulse 2, 2012
Oil on canvas and wooden frame
48 × 60 cm
Private collection

p. 27
Embrace of the Duchampian Impulse 1, 2012
Oil and spray paint on canvas and wooden frame
48 × 66 cm
Private collection

p. 29
Monumental Ecstasy, 2012
Oil on canvas and wooden frame
107 × 107 cm
Private collection

p. 30
The Ballad of Representational World, 2012
Oil on canvas and wooden frame
170 × 218 cm
Private collection

p. 31
Spatial Soother, 2012
Oil and spray paint on canvas and wooden frame
140 × 170 cm
Private collection

p. 33
Counter Balance, 2013
Oil on canvas and wooden frame
108 × 150 cm
Private collection, Germany

p. 35
Saints in a Monumental Displacement, 2013
Oil on canvas and wooden frame
144 × 174 cm
Private collection, Philippines

p. 36
Orbit, 2013
Oil and spray paint on canvas and wooden frame
110 × 80 cm
Private collection, Italy

p. 37
An Awful Ruin behind the Melting Sunrise, 2013
Oil and spray paint on canvas and wooden frame
110 × 80 cm
Private collection

p. 38
Horizontal Trap, 2013
Oil on canvas and wooden frame
110 × 80 cm
Private collection, Philippines

p. 39
Narratives of Chromophobics, 2013
Oil and spray paint on canvas and wooden frame
110 × 80 cm
Private collection, Philippines

p. 41
Before the Night Grows Old, 2015
Oil on canvas and wooden frame
71 × 56 cm
Private collection

p. 43
Fairly, Heavily, Rainbow, 2013
Oil and spray paint on canvas and wooden frame
79 × 64 cm
Private collection

p. 45
Broken Sunday, 2013
Oil on canvas and wooden frame
65 × 80 cm
Private collection, Philippines

pp. 46/47
Euphoria 1–3, 2012
Oil on canvas and wooden frame
Triptych
59 × 69 cm each
Private collection, Switzerland

p. 49
The Green, The Yellow and The Blues, 2013
Oil on canvas and wooden frame
64 × 79 cm
Private collection, Philippines

p. 50
Silent Summer, 2015
Oil and spray paint on canvas and wooden frame
71 × 56 cm

p. 51
Think Like Dead Trees, 2015
Oil and spray paint on canvas and wooden frame
132 × 102 cm

p. 53
Yellows with a Little Sense of Terror, 2014
Oil on canvas and wooden frame
40 × 35 cm
Private collection

p. 55
Sublime, 2014
Oil on canvas and wood
63 × 52 cm
Private collection

pp. 56/57
Like a Star, Hope Fell from the Heavens Below, 2014
Oil and spray paint on canvas and wooden frame
Diptych
132 × 224 cm
Private collection, Singapore

p. 59
Plane of Substantial Failure, 2014
Oil and spray paint on canvas and wooden frame
141 × 173 cm
Private collection, USA

p. 60
Landscape in the Outer Kingdom of Humanities, 2014
Oil and spray paint on canvas and wooden frame
50 × 68 cm
Private collection, Philippines

p. 61
Collapsing Constellations, 2014
Oil and spray paint on canvas and wooden frame
58 × 73 cm
Private collection

p. 62
Censored Shadow, 2014
Oil and spray paint on canvas and wooden frame
68 × 68 cm
Private collection

p. 63
Western Style, the Painter's Eye, in Fine Frenzy Rolling, 2014
Oil and spray paint on canvas and wooden frame
108 × 78 cm
The Tiroche DeLeon Collection and Art Vantage PCC Limited

p. 65
Misfortunes of the Orange Rhapsody, 2014
Oil on canvas and wooden frame
173 × 141 cm
Collection of Michael and Janet Buxton

p. 67
Desire and Sacred, 2015
Oil on canvas and wooden frame
71 × 56 cm

p. 68
This is an Apple, 2015
Oil on canvas and wooden frame
71 × 56 cm

p. 69
Off-beat, 2015
Oil on canvas and wooden frame
71 × 56 cm

p. 71
Laid Against Reality, 2015
Oil and spray paint on canvas and wooden frame
71 × 56 cm

p. 72
The Fall of Chromatic Sunrise, 2014
Oil and spray paint on canvas and wooden frame
86 × 45 cm
Private collection

p. 73
The Black and White of Yellow and Blues, 2015
Oil and spray paint on canvas and wooden frame
132 × 102 cm
Private collection, Philippines

p. 75
Be Like the Sun, Never Gone, 2015
Oil and spray paint on canvas and wooden frame
71 × 56 cm
Private collection, Philippines

p. 76
Untitled, 2014
Oil on canvas
91 × 61 cm
Private collection, USA

p. 77
Traversed, 2013
Oil on canvas and wooden frame
79 × 65 cm
Private collection, Switzerland

p. 78
Depth Against the Little Halos, 2013
Oil on canvas
44 × 34 cm
Private collection

p. 79
The Plastic Mathematics, 2013
Oil on canvas
44 × 34 cm
Private collection

p. 80
I Can't Hear the Cracklings, 2013
Oil on canvas
44 × 34 cm
Private collection

p. 81
Sempiternal Landscape, 2013
Oil on canvas
44 × 34 cm
Private collection

p. 83
Depth from the Fall of Existence, 2013
Oil on canvas
105 × 80 cm
Private collection

p. 85
Metaphorical Suffocation, 2014
Oil and spray paint on canvas, resin
176 × 140 × 78 cm
SEACO Collection

p. 86
Metaphorical Suffocation, 2014
Oil and spray paint on canvas, resin
132 × 53 × 25 cm
The Tiroche DeLeon Collection and Art Vantage PCC Limited

p. 87
Metaphorical Suffocation, 2014
Oil and spray paint on canvas, resin
173 × 70 × 40 cm
Private collection, Singapore

Jigger Cruz

1984
- Born in Malabon City, Manila, Philippines

2007
- Bachelor of Fine Arts, Far Eastern University, Manila, Philippines

Lives and works in Manila, Philippines

Selected Solo Exhibitions

2015
- *Jigger Cruz,* Arndt Berlin, Germany
- *Deep Down into the Ecstasy of False Modernism,* Primo Marella Gallery, Milan, Italy

2014
- *Overtones of Dispositional Platform,* abc art berlin contemporary, Arndt Berlin, Germany

2013
- *Grays Between Bold Parallels,* Blanc Art Space, Quezon City, Philippines
- *Depth Circus,* West Gallery, Quezon City, Philippines
- *Surface Default,* Light & Space Contemporary, Manila, Philippines

2012
- *Counter Glitch Habitation,* Primae Noctis Art Gallery, Lugano, Switzerland
- *Spatial Soother,* West Gallery, Quezon City, Philippines
- *Birth of the Party Bantam Paintings,* Secret Fresh, San Juan City, Philippines

2011
- *Dead End,* West Gallery, Quezon City, Philippines
- *Anti-Depressants on Paper,* The Crucible Gallery, Mandaluyong City, Philippines

2009
- *Constructing Deconstruction,* Tala Gallery, Quezon City, Philippines

2008
- *Swing,* Blanc Art Space, Makati City, Philippines

Selected Group Exhibitions

2014
- *Manila: The Night is Restless, The Day is Scornful,* Arndt Singapore

2013
- *Abstrakt,* Michael Haas/ Contemporary Fine Arts, Berlin, Germany
- *Water,* Taksu, Kuala Lumpur, Malaysia
- *Abstraction: Lost and Found,* Taksu, Singapore

2012
- *Latitudes. Encounters with the Philippines, Part II,* Primo Marella Gallery, Milan, Italy

2011
- *Manuel Ocampo's Boycotter of Beauty,* West Gallery, Quezon City, Philippines
- *Survivalism,* Light & Space Contemporary, Manila, Philippines
- *Thunderkiss,* Metro Gallery, San Juan City, Philippines
- *Anti-Hero,* Altro Mondo, Makati City, Philippines
- *A Soundtrack to Nothing,* The Crucible Gallery, Mandaluyong City, Philippines
- *Tanaw,* Boston Gallery, Quezon City, Philippines

2010
- *Painting with a Hammer to Nail the Crotch of Civilization,* Manila Contemporary, Taguig City, Philippines
- *Tabi Tabi Po,* 1AM Gallery, San Francisco, USA
- *Enemy,* Art Center Megamall, Mandaluyong City, Philippines
- *You Are Not Here,* Pablo Gallery, Bonifacio Global City, Taguig City, Philippines

2009
- *A Book About Death: An Unbound Book on the Subject of Death,* Emily Harvey Foundation, New York City, USA
- *If You Only Walk Long Enough,* Studio 83, Singapore
- *Looking for Juan,* Cultural Center of the Philippines, Manila, Philippines

2008
- *This Time Tomorrow,* Blanc Compound, Mandaluyong City, Philippines
- *Boxed,* Cubicle Art Space, Pasig City, Philippines

2007
- *Pink Fumes,* Pablo Gallery, Quezon City, Philippines
- *December Show,* Blanc Gallery, Makati City, Philippines
- *Opposite Attracts,* big sky mind, Quezon City, Philippines

2004–2006
- *November Rhapsody,* Art Center Megamall, Mandaluyong City, Philippines

2004
- *Philippine Art Awards,* National Museum of the Philippines, Manila, Philippines

Colophon

Editor
Matthias Arndt

Managing Editor and Editing
Kristin Rieber

Texts
Lisa Ito
Benny Nemerofsky Ramsay

Design
Bureau Mathias Beyer, Cologne

Copy Editing
Sarah Quigley

Image Editing
max-color, Berlin

Production Management
DISTANZ Verlag, Sonja Bahr

Production
optimal media GmbH, Röbel/Müritz

Photo Credits
pp. 5, 16, 17, 25–31, 78–83: Courtesy of West Gallery, Manila, photo: Luis Antonio Santos; pp. 6, 7, 59, 72: Courtesy of ARNDT Berlin/Singapore, photo: Kwan Sheung Chi; pp. 9, 50, 51, 67–71: Courtesy of ARNDT Berlin/Singapore, photo: Jigger Cruz; pp. 11, 14, 15, 77: Courtesy of Primo Marella Gallery, Milan; pp. 12/13, 46/47: Courtesy of Primae Noctis Art Gallery, Lugano, photo: Ramona Balaban; pp. 19, 20, 43: Courtesy of and photo: Jigger Cruz; pp. 21, 22/23, 53–57, 60–63, 85–87: Courtesy of ARNDT Berlin/Singapore, photo: Bernd Borchardt; pp. 33–41, 45, 73–76: Courtesy ARNDT Berlin/Singapore, photo: Olivia Kwock; p. 49: photo: Lorenzo Rufino M. Capati; p. 65: Courtesy of ARNDT Berlin/Singapore, photo: Christian Chiam

Distribution
Gestalten, Berlin
www.gestalten.com
sales@gestalten.com

ISBN 978-3-95476-108-1
Printed in Germany

Published by
DISTANZ Verlag
www.distanz.de

Cover Image
Laid Against Reality, 2015

Jigger Cruz is represented by
ARNDT Berlin/Singapore

Matthias Arndt would like to express his gratitude to Ken Hakuta, Jigger Cruz, Millicent Villanueva, Kristin Rieber, and Tobias Sirtl.